Reflections of a Grumpy Old Physician

Reflections of a Grumpy Old Physician

David A. Zohn, M.D.

VANTAGE PRESS
New York

FIRST EDITION

Published by Vantage Press, Inc.
516 West 34th Street, New York, New York 10001

Manufactured in the United States of America
ISBN: 0-533-14156-7

Library of Congress Catalog Card No.: 02-90480

0 9 8 7 6 5 4 3 2 1

Contents

Acknowledgments

I am most grateful to Richard Finkel, M.D. and Ira Seiler, M.D. for reading the manuscript and for providing helpful hints and encouragement. As always I am grateful to Norm Weiss and Curt Sandler for keeping my computer healthy and extricating me from the unending computer problems that seem to plague me. Finally, I had picked a more bland, innocuous title for the book when my daughter Sheryl selected the title I have used. I guess she knows her dad.

Introduction

I have been involved with medicine and with medical practice for the past fifty years, having started as a medical student in 1951. Even after retirement I have continued to see patients at a local university and at a free clinic. I also closely observed medicine as it was practiced in the thirties and forties for an additional twenty-plus years since my father was a physician and conducted his practice out of an office in our house—a quite common occurrence at that time. Thus I have observed and participated in medicine for most of the twentieth century. This has given me a very long-term perspective as to what medicine and medical practice is really about. To say that the changes seen in all aspects of medicine have been dramatic would be to make a vast understatement. To say that all of the problems involved with medicine and health are very complex would also be an understatement. To say that the media, the politicians and the public often attempt to make these complex issues simple is an understatement. To say that all too often painful trade-offs are necessary in the practice of medicine as well as in the economic and social spheres is likewise an understatement.

I have often been struck with how little people understand what is involved in the practice of good, modern medicine. The obvious fact that it is personalized, individualized, extremely labor intensive and technology laden would appear to explain in an evident fashion why it is so expensive, and yet people still demand the best care possible—but also as cheaply as possible. They also want perfection—a condition which cannot be found in this world. Part of the problem is the dichotomy between being healthy and being well. Most people are healthy most of the time. Therefore, during those times, they see medical costs in the form of health care insurance as a waste of money, money which could be put to much more pleasurable pursuits. However, when they become ill, there is suddenly nothing more important than their health, and hang the inconveniences of lost time and lost money. They just want to get better, with the best care possible available to them.

In these essays, I have explored the various aspects of health care as I have observed them. These range from issues pertaining to the private practice of medicine, to the practice of medicine in various types of health systems, to the larger issues of health care, including the financing aspects. Also explored are the changing attitudes and expectations of patients, the role of government in the practice of medicine, medical-legal aspects of medicine, and many others. I have also brought to your attention a number of personal experiences of mine with medicine and medical care that have stuck with me for the past fifty years. I would hope that some of these observations and experiences would resonate with other physicians. I have no doubt that many of the non-physician readers will see these problems differently, but all I can do is offer my observations and hope that you will at least keep an open mind about them.

Reflections of a Grumpy Old Physician

Health Care Issues

A Health Care Conversation

Dramatis Personae: Lowly Private Practice M.D. (L.M.D.) Lawyer, Educator, Economist, Physician Never in Private Practice (M.D.)

I read it in the newspaper. It didn't seem credible, but according to the article, the Clinton health team was proceeding with its reorganization of American medicine and American health care without the presence of even one practicing physician who runs his or her own business. In some people's minds, doctors caused the mess and should not be part of the solution. But the reorganization of health care without private practice physicians participating? Would one consider tort reform without practicing lawyers participating? If there were a problem on the shop floor would you exclude the workers there and talk instead to the President of the Union, the analyst from Wall Street and an outside accountant? What would it look like, I wondered, as a practicing physician, if I were to have a discussion with the health team members?

LAWYER: Well doctor, you are now here at the table. What thoughts about health care reform come from your perspective?
L.M.D.: I'm pleased to be able to share some thoughts with you about health care reform. It is something that

1

I, and indeed all physicians, think about on a regular basis—in actuality, for our entire professional lives. It seems clear that there are myriad problems that we face—but the problems are dominated by reconciling the control of soaring costs and the access to care of millions of uninsured with the maintenance of quality care.

LAWYER: Great. You're really not telling us anything we don't know.

L.M.D.: I hope you are not thinking of simple solutions. The problems did not develop in a simple fashion—indeed they are extraordinarily complex—and they will not be solved in a simple fashion. The first thing to realize is that there are no true villains in the piece. The closest thing to villains as a physician sees it are the trial lawyers (and more recently, the insurance companies, particularly the HMOs). However, one has to realize that they are responding to a desire on the part of the society to be made perfect or hold someone liable for it. They are semivillainous because they actively promote and encourage litigation, including new classes of litigants, for their own personal benefit rather than trying to tamp down societal desires.

M.D.: Well, what's wrong with punishing bad physicians?

L.M.D.: Absolutely nothing. First, let me say that more than anyone else, I and other practicing physicians want to see physicians who are found to be lawbreakers punished. I realize that everyone is equal before the law but physicians who violate a trust should be punished to the maximum that the law allows. The same holds true for cases of gross negligence. The problem is that most cases of perceived negligence fall into a gray area. The more potent our treatments the more effective they will be but the greater the likelihood that there will be complications and adverse outcomes. It is a trade-off that society doesn't appear to be willing to make.

EDUCATOR: Well, doctors should still be punished if they make a mistake. After all, we are talking about a human life.

L.M.D.: It is indeed a human life and we physicians have been given a sacred trust. That is why it is so painful when some physicians violate that trust. But you are talking about physicians as human beings themselves—and therefore subject to error. After all, if it is perfection you are looking for, are you willing to pay for perfection? All physicians make errors—and the longer they are in practice and the more difficult the problems they see, the more errors are likely to occur. Such errors may be either of omission or of commission. It is exceedingly painful to realize that you have made an error, but as a physician, one simply has to live with these errors and hopefully learn from them. I do not ask that we be given the right to be negligent—only the right to be human and make errors. Should these errors be investigated? Of course! Should some system of compensation be set up for patients? Of course! But do you really expect your physician to be absolutely right and absolutely perfect all the time, or do you wish him to be honest with you and try his or her best at all times?

Look at it another way, if every act performed on a patient—for example a procedure, a prescription written, an examination performed, medicines given by a health professional, etc. can be considered a transaction, literally millions of transactions take place each day and perhaps billions each year. Given the sheer enormity of these transactions, it is a wonder that so many things go right—not that anything goes wrong.

LAWYER: Let's get back to the major problems. First and foremost, cost, since health dollars are eating up a larger and larger part of our GDP.

L.M.D.: Of course you are right. After all, I am a consumer as well as a provider and each month I have to write those monstrous health insurance checks. But the causes of escalating costs are multiple and many reside outside of the health care system. For example problems relating to drug abuse, crime, alcohol abuse and related highway problems, tobacco use and many others are sociological problems beyond the control of physicians. These represent billions of dollars in unnecessary health costs. The nature of health care, too, has changed dramatically. It used to be episodic and acute, and many of the non-infectious diseases such as coronary artery disease, cancer and stroke were rapidly fatal. Now new techniques have improved survival but have necessitated prolonged longitudinal care. Also, technology has evolved markedly, bringing enormous benefits as well as unhappy side effects. Then, too, there are structural problems in the delivery of care with administrative costs, defensive medicine and over-specialization playing a role.

ECONOMIST: We know that physicians' fees and their ordering of tests is what drives up costs. This is what we need to control if we are to get a handle on the macroeconomic picture of health care costs.

L.M.D.: Macro schmacro—physicians see patients one by one, each with a different set of needs that must be addressed. Further, you have made several statements and several implications that need to be discussed individually. The first applies to physician's fees, which you imply are far too high. The median income of physicians at this time is $159,000 ½ higher, ½ lower. This figure is predicated on a sixty-hour week so it is much less if you consider the norm to be a forty-hour week. The average is significantly higher than that because there are a number of specialists who make very big incomes. But think

4

about it for a minute. Nobody has a longer education and training program than physicians. They spend, after college, four years in medical school and four to six years in postgraduate training after that. Many come out heavily in debt. Considering the amount of time spent in education and training, and the unique responsibility that they bear, is that really such a wild income? How do you expect to attract top quality students, ask them to give up a decade of their life, and go into debt to boot, and then begrudge them a decent living? If young people were primarily interested in financial rewards rather than service, going through medical school and residency training seems a funny way to go about it. Why not get an M.B.A. or an L.L.B. in a fraction of the time and at a fraction of the cost and then go directly into business or Wall Street? My own personal opinion is that physicians should become wealthy from marrying money, inheriting money or investing money, but not from medical practice. However, I absolutely feel that physicians should earn a very comfortable living and should not be made a whipping boy for a complex problem that they did not create. Are there abusers of the system whose primary concern is greed? Unfortunately the answer is "yes" but aren't they a mirror of a society whose only way to count is a person's net worth? We used to respect learning, wisdom, kindness and many other virtues, but now we seem to bow only to the bottom line. Finally, a physician's fees make up less than 20 percent of health care costs. Even if cut by 15 or 20 percent (and I am not convinced that it is at all desirable or feasible to do that), we would save only 1 to 2 percent of our total health care budget. But in answer to your comment, it is true that ordering procedures for outpatients as well as in patients does make up a larger proportion of the health care dollar. These tests, however,

5

are essential to the early and accurate diagnosis of illnesses—so that now we can treat these problems far better than before, when we had to wait for the gross manifestations of disease to appear.

EDUCATOR: Yes, and we know that physicians own facilities and send patients to those facilities for profit.

L.M.D.: Everything is more complicated than it seems to be on the surface. Let's look at why physicians order procedures. As a medical student, one is taught to be a scientist and to follow the scientific method. As a resident and/or fellow, the emphasis is on the thoroughness of the work-up and the ruling out of all possibilities before the diagnosis is made. Woe betide the resident who fails to order a serum porcelain test on the presentation of the case during hospital rounds. When in practice, one wishes to continue the methods used in training. During training, one learns to perform various procedures and it is only natural to want to use those procedures in the course of one's work. Everyone wants to look like an up-to-date modern practitioner employing the latest technologies.

But it doesn't end there. Patients come to the office and apply pressure to have one or more tests performed. It is not pure weakness on the part of the physician to give in to patients. These are procedures he routinely performs (or uses) and of course they seem perfectly reasonable to him. Further, most of medicine is a gray area. Something *could* be there which a test would reveal—or reveal earlier. And then of course there is always the specter of how it looks if a procedure has not been performed and something is missed. In our society, one can be reasonably certain that a lawsuit will follow and that the physician will be defenseless if a test is not performed and the diagnosis not made.

It is perfectly true that some physicians set up joint ventures and then over-refer to the facility, but many times the facility is set up for other reasons—e.g. for convenience, or because such a service is not readily available. Most of the time the referrals are used appropriately, but it is certainly true that abuses do occur. Physicians were very foolish when they believed the government, and particularly the Federal Trade Commission, which told them that they should stop acting like professionals employing cottage industry techniques and instead should become entrepreneurs and businessmen—advertise, market, band together, deliver services in a new way and compete. The old restraints of professional behavior and peer censorship were thrown off and competition became rampant with many of the side effects of competition. So you can see that there are many pressures on a physician to perform or order a procedure and precious few not to. The current buzzword is cognitive functions—more thinking and less doing—which is fine except that as modern offices (with modern overhead) are set up, cognitive functions will not even pay the overhead, let alone earn a living. If some of these pressures could be removed and physicians allowed to behave as professionals, the upward pressure on cost of procedures might be dampened; however, they will not be reversed, because modern medicine does perform miracles—but at a cost.

I would like to remind everyone here that this is abstract (how can billions of dollars be concrete?) and philosophical but when you are ill, you wish nothing but the best and hang the cost. To detour for a second, I see three classes of patients. The first is the worried well where a careful history and physical examination, perhaps a few simple tests and some reassurance will not necessitate significant additional costs. These patients may be cost conscious and may be willing to forego procedures (particularly if they have not met their deductible). The second category is those who have a self-limited problem—a problem which is annoying or even painful, but not life-threatening or likely to result in a disability. These patients need more care and attention but are still aware of costs and are willing to wait. The third category is the patient with a serious illness or injury. All thoughts of cost go out the window. In all my years of practice, I have never had a patient with one of the latter problems ask for the cheapest surgeon, the cheapest consultant or the cheapest hospital. None has ever asked me not to do a procedure that I felt necessary. So costs are the concern of the healthy, and wellness is the concern of the ill. This is not just a modern concern. (continued on p. 13)

Illustrations
Plus ça change, plus c'est la même chose (the more things change the more they are the same). The four medieval prints by the artist Egbert von Panderen and Hendrik Goltzius illustrate the four stages of illness and the reaction of patients to their physician during each stage. Although the prints were done in the Middle Ages, these reactions seem to have changed very little if at all in current times.

During the acute stage of the illness, the physician is seen as God. After the acute stage has passed and it appears that the patient will recover, the physician is seen as an Angel. During convalescence, the physician is seen as a man—a wise and learned man, but nevertheless a man. Finally, complete recovery has taken place and

Figure A: Allegorical figure of the physician as God. Interior view with three scenes: patient in bed being treated by surgeon, nurse and an assistant; woman drying bandages (?) at a fire-place; another bedside scene. Praying plays a prominent role.

Figure B: Allegorical figure of the physician as an Angel standing among books and tools of the medical profession. Interior scene: two views of patients in bed consulting with physicians; splint being replaced on broken leg; woman with small pot at fireplace.

HG. excud.
3 Famâ Machaonia magis et magis arte leuatus,   ΙΑΤΡΟΣ ΠΟΛΛΩΝ   O HOMO, non frustrà tantos subysse labores
Cum sedet ante focum, progrediturue tripes.   ΑΝΤΑΞΙΟΣ ΑΛΛΩΝ.   Nosces; quod restat tu modò tolle malum.

Figure C: Allegorical figure of the physician as a Man standing among books and tools of the medical profession. Interior view: surgery patient is having bandages changed; man with broken leg is on crutches; and the third patient is sitting by the fireplace.

Aſt ego ſi penitus iam ſanum pristinia poſcam, ΥΒΡΙΣ ΤΕ ΚΑΙ ΠΛΗΓΗ Cautior exemplo tu DVM DOLET ACCIPE, noſtro,
Ille Deus pridem mox ÇACODÆMON ero . ΑΝΤΙ ΣΩΣΤΡΩΝ . Qui Medice exerres gnauiter artis opus .

Figure D: Allegorical figure of the physician as the Devil standing among books and tools of the medical profession. Interior view, two scenes: the patients have recovered fully and the physician has come to collect his fee.

now the physician presents his bill. Now he is seen as the Devil.

LAWYER: That's all very fine, but we must control costs one way or the other.

L.M.D.: It will probably be the other (just joking). Seriously, when we talk about controlling costs, in the back of our minds we are gambling that we will stay healthy. If not, we are gambling that we will be able to find our way in the system and obtain the care that we feel we need. As for the rest of them out there—we will be back to the layering of care. When I started in medicine there were definite layers of care. The wealthy were able to fend for themselves and seek out the best care available. The poor were taken care of at municipal hospitals (which were often staffed by university people) and on the teaching wards of private hospitals. Care was provided primarily by resident physicians with supervision by attending physicians, and although often not outstanding, it usually was pretty good. As usual, the middle class was left to fend for itself—doing the best it could. With the advent of near universal insurance and in particular, Medicare, care given to middle class and upper class people flattened out, being the same in essentials. Of course, the wealthy could afford private rooms, private nurses, special dining facilities, etc., but the basic quality of care was the same. Now we seem to be going back to a layering, particularly between the middle and upper classes. The latter will get the care and attention it needs from private physicians, even if it means going to a clinic in Switzerland or a hospital set up on a luxurious Caribbean island. The middle class will again make do: a stripped down HMO for basic care, the selection of a private physician when there seems to be a need, etc.

M.D.: Come on doctor, HMOs provide pretty good care, don't they?

L.M.D.: I'm sure they vary, as do individual physicians, but the premise of an HMO, which has a capitation fee, is *not* providing care—that is where they make a profit, usually divided up amongst the providers at the end of the year. There is really nothing wrong with making a profit—we are after all a capitalist country, and we know that that is a very strong motivator—but HMO's may provide too few services just as private physicians are thought to provide too many.

ECONOMIST: Perhaps what we need is a health care system such as exists in Canada where a global budget is agreed to and the dividing of the pie is done between the physician and the provincial government.

L.M.D.: People used to say that the system they wished to emulate was that of Britain, but now it is that of Canada. I wonder why? Not really. The twentieth century has revealed the weaknesses of malignant socialism (Germany, Russia) and benign socialism (Britain, Sweden, Israel) as engines to motivate people and drive the economy. These weaknesses become apparent only over many decades and apply to health care systems as well.

I strongly suspect that the same will be true of Canada's health care system; indeed it is already starting. If, in a global budget, one runs out of money, one simply transfers money from the capital account (building of new facilities) to the operating account (provision of care). That is all right for a year or two, but if it goes on for many years, the facilities face obsolescence and rationing of care becomes more pronounced. The same is true for the institution of new procedures and the use of new technologies. The two are delayed or rationed (a fortunate

14

gift for U.S. hospitals near the Canadian border that handle the overflow). Pressure is put on physicians to hold down their fees and this leads to a great deal of physician disaffection (I personally would rather be treated by a happy and contented physician) and gradually the energy of the system is directed into warfare between competing groups rather than where it belongs—providing good patient care.

EDUCATOR: In spite of what you say, we may come to a total reform of the health care system in which the government is sole provider (universal care). With modern technologies we can save huge sums on administrative costs and pass them on to the health care consumer.

L.M.D.: In theory you certainly can. Whether you will or not in a government system is unclear since health care is a bottomless pit and there will be enormous pressure on government to expand the coverage provided. We are not flying blind, however, since we have a large number of government medicine systems in place—the Veteran's Administration, military medicine, the Public Health Service, state, county and municipal hospitals, etc. It is not necessary to get into a debate about the quality of the care provided by these government services, only to note that people are not clamoring to be included in them, and I believe that people show their true intentions with their feet, not their mouths.

I can't help but believe, however, that there is another element involved in those who propose universal health insurance provided by the Federal Government. Being ill means losing control of one's body, and to strangers at that. One way of maintaining control is by making the doctor your servant, and not (temporarily) your master. It is just a theory.

ECONOMIST: One way to save money would be to have a greater number of primary care physicians. Don't you agree?

L.M.D.: I do indeed. Here, too, it is not a case of wickedness or evil intent that has led to a drop in the number of primary physicians, but a complex series of events. Hospitals do not emphasize primary care training for a variety of reasons: relative lack of demand by medical students, lack of research potential in the clinically oriented fields of primary care, the low regard for teaching as compared to research and writing, the lower likelihood of obtaining large scale grants which provide facilities and staff as well as funds for research and the relatively low usage of expensive equipment by primary care physicians as compared to specialists. Young doctors do not go into primary care fields because they leave medical school in debt and primary care does not pay as well as it should. Also, they do not have the respect from either patients or fellow physicians that they clearly deserve. Physicians do enter specialty or subspecialty fields because there is a knowledge explosion leading to learning more and more about less and less. Physicians want to use what truly are new and dazzling technologies and interventions (it is interesting to see the blurring of the line between interventional non-surgeons and surgeons, but the end result is the use of more technology). They also want greater respect from colleagues and patients, and last, but not least, more money. This is really unfortunate since so many problems can be managed by primary care doctors in a more cost effective and yet good quality way. Something has to be figured out to encourage more primary care medicine based on lower reimbursement for the performing of procedures.

M.D.: I want to go back to the concept of universal health care coverage for a moment. Under that system, physicians would be on a salary, but don't you think that even so they will act professionally and provide quality care? Isn't that what we were trained to do?

LMD.: Sure. Those patients seen will be given good care—to do anything less would be unprofessional. The question is—how many will be seen? If you are on a salary, why bother working in an additional patient? If it is not an emergency, they can wait, and if it is an emergency, that is what the emergency room clinic is for. Why come in early, miss your lunch hour or stay late to see additional patients? Of course, if it is a fascinoma (medicalese for interesting medical problem) or a V.I.P. you will somehow squeeze them in but otherwise why bother? Why bother to come back from vacation early to take care of paperwork so that it won't interfere with office hours? Why sit in an office and see patients when you can be attending an interesting medical conference? Further, with income fixed, attention is directed towards peripheral matters—how many days for vacation, for attendance at medical meetings, what is the quota of patients that must be seen, etc.

LAWYER: I don't see many helpful suggestions here for cost control. All you do is shoot down every suggestion raised.

L.M.D.: That's not true. I believe that many things can be done to control costs. I haven't gotten into that because I know that you also want to discuss access for those without health insurance.

LAWYER: That's correct. Don't you think that access is important?

L.M.D.: I do indeed. There, is of course, access through municipal and county health clinics, school health clinics and municipal and county hospitals, but the provision of insurance for the 35 million uninsured or underinsured (Medicaid) would certainly be desirable. How to do it is the question. It's certainly not credible that it can be done at no cost. To my mind, some limited access via a hierarchy of treatment methods seems appropriate.

EDUCATOR: That's certainly not fair and not the American way.

L.M.D.: I don't know about the American way, but we must discuss the concept of fairness. Traditionally, the three concerns of health care provision have been cost, access and quality. If you throw in fairness, that guarantees that no solution will ever be found because there will be eternal squabbling about what can be considered to be fair. The more productive way to look at it would be to say that we are a just society, and as such intend for all citizens to be entitled to food in their belly, clothing on their back and a roof over their head. We do not demand in the name of fairness that everyone eat the same food, wear the same clothing and live in the same kind of house. If we use the paradigm of education—free public education for all who want it—we can talk all we want to about fairness and equality, but we know that more affluent school districts are going to provide (one way or another) the necessary extras that make a quality education. Is it fair? Perhaps not, but it certainly is reality.

I will briefly propose a way to provide quality care to those who do not currently have it, without enormous bureaucratic costs. I would establish fifty-one foundations (see Medical Foundations), one for each state, and a national one, all of which would be chartered as quasi-governmental tax-exempt entities. That means that they would be able to accept charitable contributions, both in cash and in kind. They would be able to set up endowment funds and encourage individuals and corporations to make donations. They would be able to raise funds the same way. The role of the small national foundation would be to set minimal standards of care to be provided by all foundations and to disseminate information as to what each foundation is doing. Above the minimum, each state would be able to concentrate on what is seen as its own needs. New York may choose AIDS whereas West Virginia or Kentucky might choose Black Lung Disease, etc. An important feature would be the establishment of clinics throughout the state. There would be a permanent staff, but it would be supplemented by retired health care professionals who will donate their time (undoubtedly on the condition that liability insurance be provided). This would include not only physicians, but also dentists, nurses, therapists, etc. Some equipment could be donated by hospitals and by physicians, drugs by pharmacies and pharmaceutical companies, etc. It is simply an expansion of the various free clinics that exist throughout the country without markedly expanding the bureaucracy. Would it work? I don't know, but a small pilot program could certainly be set up.

LAWYER: At least we are seeing some answers and not just knocking down everything else. What do you see as our solution to the problem of cost?

L.M.D.: Before we talk about what's wrong and how to fix it, let's not forget to talk about what's right. All of our health care providers are well trained and of high quality. People from all over the world still come to American institutions to be trained and to be treated. This was not always so. This is primarily a post-World War II phenomenon. We don't spend much time talking about quality because we have it and have come to expect it. Most of our patients, most of the time, get high quality care; most of our patients, most of the time, are pleased with their own physicians. Everyone complains about the cost, but one must not forget there are psychological factors at work—being ill is both unpleasant and a waste of money, money that could be better spent on pleasurable matters. We mustn't forget our remarkable pharmaceutical, biotechnology and medical equipment industry. It certainly fits the bill as the kind of industry we want to promote in this country. It is high tech, provides high quality jobs and is a heavy exporter. If specific members of the industry have done something wrong they should be punished—but if not, why make a scapegoat of one of our premier industries? It is true that costs are high (virtually all of the drugs and equipment we use today are new since I started practicing medicine—an enormous accomplishment) in no small part due to the costs of defending against litigation; however, when I go to the pharmacy, I consider what I am paying a subsidy to improve the health of my children and grandchildren as well as helping to keep a vital American industry competitive. For the same reason I try, if possible, to buy American cars rather than imports.

Now for what needs to be done. Societal reform would be first on my list. Much of health care is demand driven and society must learn to damp down its demands. Physicians cannot see patients until they actually walk in the door. There are limits as to what can be done for people. Not only must expectations of perfection be lowered, but also people must take responsibility for their own actions. An example of this is a suit against tobacco companies for the contraction of cancer from smoking. I happen to believe that cigarette smoking is a pernicious habit which causes a wide range of health problems and I would have no problem with heavy taxation on tobacco products, or even their outright abolition, but for patients with tobacco-related illnesses to blame someone else for their own behavior is ingenuous at best, and destructive of individual responsibility at worst. It is also a good example of trial lawyers constantly seeking to widen the range of torts that can be brought to litigation. A large portion of our society is dysfunctional, with rampant drug and alcohol abuse, crime, and failure to take minimal preventive measures for a variety of health problems. These factors are outside the range of health care but have a strong impact on health care costs (and societal costs as well).

Next on my list is tort reform. This is true both in general and with regard to professional liability. By general tort reform I refer to product liability and accident cases. Nobody in the world has a system like ours that is staggering in its cost implications and largely demand driven. As a physician, I want the right to be wrong (to make an honest mistake), but not the right to be negligent. All cases where negligence is alleged should be brought before a binding arbitration panel. If one side or the other is unhappy with the results, they can move to a trial by jury. But the results of arbitration must be presented in court and the losing side pays the court fees. Sitting on these arbitration panels should be retired judges, lawyers and physicians. There is an underutilized pool of wise and talented people: retirees with no axes to grind whose services in these and other matters would greatly reduce costs.

Structural reforms in the delivery of care are necessary. Because we are a large and varied country, there is room for the provision of many kinds of service: prepaid plans (HMOs or PPOs), large multispecialty groups, single specialty groups and solo practitioners. But whatever the method of practice, all health care professionals need relief from the pressure of rising overhead that must inevitably be passed to the patient. Lowering liability malpractice insurance is one large way to control costs that can be accomplished by tort reform.

Health insurance reform is essential. There are between 900 and 1500 insurance firms delivering a health care package each with its own forms and its own unique way of annoying consumers and providers alike. The micromanagement of decision making, the deliberate delay in payment to keep the float going, and the wide variety of forms make practicing a nightmare. A single universal insurance form is a necessity. I would gather together all appropriate representatives of third party payers, providers and consumers and set up criteria for rating the companies much like the Guide Michelin. This, together with a listing of the twenty-five best and twenty-five worst companies would be distributed (free of cost) in every post office in the country. I believe the fall in the number of companies would be dramatic as well as the rise in the quality of service.

I would like to see a return to professionalism in physicians. They are not entrepreneurs and not businessmen (by and large they are lousy at both) but professionals. Professionals do not advertise and do not openly compete. Society should be willing to make a bargain with physicians: We will treat you as professional people, allow you to discipline and regulate your own without the eternal fear of litigation provided you are seen to be acting in the best interests of society and your patients and not simply your own selfish interests. If not, we will take away your privilege and regulate you like a giant public utility. Lastly, I feel that the Medicare problem must be addressed. Those who can afford it will simply have to pay for a larger share of medical insurance or will have to obtain supplemental insurance of their own, or both.

LAWYER: Any other suggestions?

L.M.D.: I would go about your task with two features—a sense of humor and an enormous sense of humility.

Death Technicians

The debate about the treatment of pre-terminal and terminal illness grows louder as our population ages. A new right has been discovered: the right to die—not by one's hand, but under the active hand of the physician. It is true that a dying patient presents an extraordinarily difficult time for the patient, the family and for the care-givers. However, involving the physician in the process of active euthanasia seems to me to be a grave mistake. The physician's role is to preserve life to the fullest extent possible. Failing that, it should be to make the patient as comfortable as possible. As performed currently, a quiet conspiracy takes place when the patient is terminal and clearly near the end. This takes place between the physicians, nursing staff, family, and of course, the patient (if lucid). To relieve pain and make the patient comfortable, large quantities of opiates are administered. If they should happen to depress respiration and cause the patient's demise, then man has simply assisted nature. This is a private matter and in no way a public policy issue.

A right to die law cannot help but lead to major problems for physicians, and in a larger sense, for all patients as well. The distinction between physician-as-healer and physician-as-killer will blur, to the benefit of no one. Initially there will be stringent rules in place, but with time and practicality, these will tend to erode. Personal judgment ("there is no quality of life") will intrude. Several years ago, the *Journal of the American Medical Association (JAMA)* featured a brief article called "Good-Bye Debbie," in which a resident on call came across a patient in the terminal stages of ovarian cancer. He did not know the patient at all, and yet, without consultation, he used a lethal dose of opiates. The coarseness exhibited by the resident physician would surely become magnified with time. Patients would never be sure, particularly those with debilitating or chronic illnesses, whether their physician will function as healer or executioner.

Pressure from the family also comes into play ("doctor, stop him/her from suffering") and this may adversely affect the behavior of the physicians. It seems to me that however well motivated a physician may be in this matter, the action taken by him, often under pressure, can produce a coarsening of the role of the physician.

Pain and depression for the most part can be adequately treated, and in a non-sterile humane environment. This is the lesson of hospice. However, if release from this world is requested, or if the right to die becomes law, the physician should not be directly involved in the active cause of the demise. Rather, a new class of technicians should be put in place—death technicians. After all it is technicians who perform lethal injections when public executions take place. Doctor Jack Kevorkian is really a technician when he performs lethal acts. He is certainly not functioning as a physician. In a prior life he was a pathologist; thus, he had no live patient contact or experience. As seen in a video he produced, he barely knows the patient, asks only the most superficial questions and does not attempt palliation.

Technicians run all the complex diagnostic testing that exists in hospitals. Surely protocols can be developed which, when followed, will result in the death of the patient. Please don't involve the physicians.

Government Medicine

It is often proposed that the current system in which insurance is provided via employment or via Medicare be scrapped and a single payer system—i.e. the Federal government—be instituted. It was my fortune (misfortune ?) to be associated with three separate government agencies which were providing medical care. Let me share some of my experiences with you.

The first and by far the best was military medicine (Navy). The mission of the Medical Corps was to take care of the troops—the sailors and marines. That came first, and that, by and large, was done well. However, some less than ideal medicine was practiced in other situations. Every week, two (sometimes three) physicians would take care of over a hundred recruits—in a morning. Needless to say, all attention was paid to the presenting symptom and zero attention to the individual. Indeed, all were examined and treated together in one large examining room with absolutely no privacy. Although no one intended it, the practice reminded me of a cattle car. Officers were of course treated much better.

I recall one instance in which a physician who was second in command in his department and the head of the department residency training program had a run-in with the commanding officer. Within forty-eight hours he was aboard a carrier in the Pacific. So much for meeting vital medical needs when they came up against military needs. Dependents needed to be taken care of, and they were, in a fashion. Dependents clinics were staffed on a rotation basis by all physicians on base. It would be perfectly possible for an ophthalmologist to treat gynecologic problems and a gynecologist to treat allergies. Certainly less than optimal care. Finally, most physicians did their best to provide care, but no one went out of their way looking for extra work. Compared with what I later observed in private practice significantly less work was performed by military physicians. All in all, however, military medicine was by far the best of the lot in the government care systems I observed.

Medicine as practiced in the Veterans Administrative (VA) was next—and a large step down. People followed the letter, but not the spirit of the law (rules). They had to report at 8 A.M. and they did, but then adjourned to the coffee shop until 8:50 A.M. so they could begin work at 9 A.M. At 11:30 A.M. they stopped work to get ready for lunch. Between 3:30 and 4 P.M. work stopped for the day. They could not leave until 4:45 P.M. so there was constant and incessant chatter, primarily about one topic—what they would do when they retired. This would include not just short-termers but people with eight–ten years to go until retirement. All would have calendars on which they crossed off the weeks and months. Care provided the patients was not terrible, but neither was it great. Mediocrity would best describe the care.

Further, there were always political considerations. The following year's budget depended upon the current years' number of admissions. If, towards the end of the year they appeared to be coming up short of projections, the word went out and everyone who came into the general outpatient clinic found himself in a hospital bed, whether he expected to be or not. Discharging patients was a problem, too, since the fore and aft cap boys (representatives of the American Legion, Veterans of Foreign Wars, etc.) would have to pass on such a discharge if a patient complained. Often times an appropriate discharge was countermanded because one of the vets, and his lobbyists, objected.

Far and away the worst of all three that I observed was the large municipal hospital where I toiled for five long years. It is difficult to describe how poor the care was, and how difficult it was to provide any semblance of good care. I recall that we waited for two years to get an IBM Selectric typewriter (at that time the state of the art in typewriters, if you remember what those were) for the secretarial staff. We finally got it, but it was on a Friday afternoon and it was not bolted to the desk. When we returned on Monday morning it was gone. By the end of the month, the hospital would have run out of everything, including vital medicines such as antibiotics. I recall seeing staff wiping patients with sheets because they had run out of towels. Laboratory studies were either late or lost. A large amount of a resident's time was spent trying to track down errant x-rays, wheeling people to various laboratory studies so they would be done in a reasonable time frame and cajoling hospital staff to do the report in something like a timely fashion. The gift shop was staffed by the Lighthouse for the Blind and was robbed regularly. Many of the patients were not terribly helpful. They would not take their prescribed medicines and would not keep clinic appointments. Even worse, pregnant females would not avail themselves of pre-natal care and would be seen for the first time during delivery, at which time diabetes, pre-eclampsia and other major health problems would be uncovered. I recall two patients, one with an amputation and the other with burns, brought into the hospital, not because of their terrible Staphylococcus infections but because of the smell from the untreated infections. They did nothing about these overwhelming infections until neighbors brought them in. Patients would regularly sell the equipment we gave them (prostheses, crutches, wheel chairs) and return for more.

If working with the patients was difficult, the administration was worse. One had to wait months just to meet with the administrator, and many months more to get a decision about a needed improvement—often a "no," due to budgetary restrictions. Turf wars were fierce. A meeting requiring perhaps five–six people would have thirty, as each department head was there to protect his turf. Planning (scheming) was constantly going on as to how to acquire more beds, more staffing slots, more clinic time, etc. Needless to say, it was a zero-sum game, with winners and losers, so the battle was fierce.

Why did physicians stay in such a hostile environment? Many were hired by the local medical schools to teach interns and residents, which they enjoyed doing. Those who were not university affiliated practiced a common stratagem. The hospital pretended to pay them and they pretended to work. That would last only so long and then they were gone.

For those who blithely propose a single-payer universal health care system, the above mini-description of life in various government agencies should make them think twice, and then thrice, about such an idea.

Health Care—A Bottomless Pit

Health care is indeed a bottomless pit. Whether we are talking about prevention, diagnosis, treatment or long term care, the amount of care available, and desired, is truly without limit. And without limit as to cost as well. Therefore, what to pay for and what not, is a matter of intense dispute.

The recent dispute about Viagra is typical. When some insurance companies paid for some impotent men to take Viagra, women's groups complained that contraception should also be covered. It appears not to have dawned upon any of them that perhaps neither are medical emergencies nor are they medical necessities and perhaps neither should be compensated. It would seem to me that these are non-health threatening events (albeit improving the quality of life—but then again so does cosmetic plastic surgery, much of mental health, massage and relaxation therapy, herbal therapy and many, many others). The payment for each of these should be made on an individual basis and cost should largely, if not entirely, be borne by the individual.

Several factors come into play. First, naturally, everyone wants his or her problem to be covered by insurance. This is, to them, essential care, but for other people, the needs and desires of these individuals are driving up the costs of health care by non-essential usage. Second, people hold the irrational belief that they are simply entitled to more care and to better care, all of course cheaper—an obvious impossibility.

To demonstrate how difficult this problem is, I believe that all would agree that catastrophic illness is a problem that is deserving of insurance coverage. But what if the treatment is an experimental treatment, for which clear-cut benefits have not as yet been demonstrated? And what if the treatment is extraordinarily expensive so that one could say, for example, that a large number of children could be vaccinated or home health care could be provided to a large number of the elderly for that amount of money? I do not know the answer to the problem, but I do know that there is no easy way to decide how to allocate health resources. Choices will have to be made. Further, we will have to pay more money in insurance costs to permit us to make some of these choices.

Nobody enjoys paying out money for health problems. They would far rather pay money for pleasurable things. However, we as a community should realize that we are a wealthy society, that enormous sums are paid each year for non-essentials such as entertainment, dining out, cosmetics, etc., not to mention illicit drug use. Surely we as a society could afford to pay a slightly greater amount of money (and a slightly higher percentage of Gross Domestic Product [G.D.P.]) to have a wider coverage of important health needs. What we must insist upon is that the moneys are used wisely and prudently.

Insurance companies, HMOs, and the like are, for the most part, profit-making organizations and they and their shareholders certainly deserve to make such a profit on their investment. They are also in the health business and have to realize that that puts certain constraints on the amount of profit that they earn. Perhaps a limit should be imposed—high enough to satisfy shareholders but not without a ceiling. This might be something like the pre-deregulation era utility companies in which a rate commission set the amount of increases allowable. Those who do not wish to be limited can drop out of the health business. There seem to be more than enough insurance companies around in the health care business. If not enough, perhaps a quasi-public insurance company can be set up, one which would be eligible for charitable contributions.

We as a society have to get used to the idea that there is no free lunch and that one way or another things have to be paid for. To expect quality care without paying for it is an impossible dream. To not realize that health care is a bottomless pit and that in some ways we have to decide what it is that we will pay for is to ignore reality.

Medical Care as a Right

Medical care is claimed to be an inalienable right which should not only be available to all, but on an absolutely equal basis. To me that shows wrong terminology leading to a wrong concept. The correct concept to me is that we are striving to be a just society, and as such a society, people in need should look forward to having their basic health care needs taken care of.

The problem arises when the claim is made for "equal" care, whatever that means. An analogy can be made that as a just society we do not wish people—any people—to be without food, clothing or shelter. It can readily be seen that, although we do not wish to have people starving in the street, shivering in the cold, or going without a roof over their heads, nobody claims that we must all eat the same food, wear the same clothing or live in the same style house. We recognize that there are going to be some differences, as we should recognize in medical care as well.

It is the feeling of some that the Federal government should be the provider of all health care. The idea of a single bureaucracy managing $\frac{1}{7}$ of the GDP does not seem to bother some people. What a super bureaucracy that would be—larger than the Pentagon, without doubt the largest bureaucracy in the country. Couple that single address with the absolutely bottomless pit of health care, and you have a situation in which politics will surely prevail. This or that program or procedure will be included based on political and not health care reasons. Further, expenses will rise far higher and faster than expected—always. There will be many reasons for this phenomenon including an aging population, exploding new technology, higher costs of doing business, etc. These rising costs can only be met by some combination of limited payouts (to the health providers, but certainly not the administrators), by raising taxes and by rationing care. For those who believe in full equality of care for all, consider that the wealthy will figure out a way to get the care that they believe they need and the poor will be left behind. If one needed an example of what Federal medical care would look like, one need go no further than the VA system. Care is not terrible, nor is it superior (with the exception of a few areas such as tropical diseases, amputations, spinal cord injuries and burns). It is really about mediocrity. One need look only at the behavior of veterans themselves. If they can afford private care, they use it rather than the free care provided by the VA. The idea that patients would be admitted in order to bolster the next year's fiscal budget, not being discharged from the hospital because an American Legion or VFW representative objects is preposterous, but it happens frequently. To sum up the system, ones does not hear of non-veterans clamoring to get into the system, do you?

It is generally recognized that there are three components to health care. These are quality, access and cost. Quality varies from institution to institution as well as from practitioner to practitioner. Minimal standards are maintained by means of approval by recognized certifying organizations for both hospitals and medical schools, recertification of hospitals at fixed intervals, licensure exams for physicians and other health care providers, Specialty Board Exams for residents who have completed their training, recertification for physicians, continuing education requirements for all health practitioners, etc. However, it should be recognized that quality still varies greatly from institution to institution and from practitioner to practitioner. There is no way that everyone will obtain exactly the same quality of care. Access likewise varies greatly, depending upon geography and upon the facilities available in the neighborhood. Cost is obviously a significant variable. The more services provided, the higher the cost. If those costs cannot be met through insurance coverage or individual payments, then the wherewithal to continue the services disappears and so does the service. And ultimately so does the quality. And the access.

It is really not as if there is a complete absence of care for the impoverished, although it is often stated or implied that that is so. The number of people without insurance is often mentioned as showing that these people do not get essential health care. Most just cannot afford it or do not work where it (health care insurance) is provided. However, it should not be forgotten that within that number are individuals who are capable of paying the premium but are gambling that they are healthy, will stay that way, and therefore will not have to pay for the insurance. Lack of insurance is obviously a handicap to readily obtaining care, but there is in place throughout the country a large network of facilities to take care of the indigent. There are municipal or county hospitals or both in all cities in this country which provide care for the needy. These municipalities have a network of Outpatient clinics as well as Home Health services. All teaching hospitals have not only inpatient facilities for the needy but Outpatient facilities as well. The states have a network of mental health facilities (IP and OP), while the Federal government provides health care to service personnel and their dependents as well as the VA, where any veteran can obtain health care. The Federal government also has a Public Health Service which has IP and OP facilities, and which serves needy people, most notably American Indians who live on reservations. There is a growing network of Free Clinics, staffed by volunteers, lay and professional, including large numbers of retired physicians. I have suggested elsewhere (see "Foundations") another approach to provide health care to the needy.

Well, you say, what about the quality of care provided? It varies. There are many dedicated health professionals who staff these clinics and hospitals, including medical residents, whose devotion to their patients often exceeds that of the private practitioner. The question I would ask is: "What is the responsibility of the patient?" I recall quite vividly the comments by the Chief of Ob/Gyn at the local municipal hospital where I worked that all too many women came to delivery with absolutely no pre-natal care, although of course it was available to them. Many of these women would arrive with serious, even life-threatening illnesses. I also recall very well two individuals who were brought in with overwhelming infections. They did not come in by themselves but were brought in by neighbors because of the overwhelming smell of putrefaction. I treated patients with spinal cord injuries (SCI) obtained during drug wars. I fitted people with canes, crutches, wheel chairs and artificial limbs only to find out that they were promptly sold for cash. Medicines prescribed were not taken. This half of the equation is never mentioned although individual responsibility is an essential component of health care.

Equal care means equal access and equal quality. Does it also mean equal cost? If so, where in the world is the money going to come from, except from higher taxes, which will lead to economic stagnation and probably to recession. The fundamental problem is that health care is a bottomless pit. There simply is not enough money in this country to provide for everything that people think they want and need. Therefore choices must be made.

It is not being cruel but rather realistic to state that in any society, rich people have better access to their needs than do poor people. Even in societies which were presumably ruled by egalitarianism, such as communism, layering of society and the services provided to various classes of society takes place—well described in George Orwell's *Animal Farm*, where all animals were equal but some animals were more equal than others. An effort to strengthen the various health components providing care to the needy is desirable. An effort to provide absolutely equal care for all is bound to fail.

Therefore, we must restate our goals. Instead of insisting on "fairness" and "full equality of health care for all," we should emphasize that we are a just society which will make every effort to provide quality care to all of its citizens. But it should be remembered that that is a goal, not necessarily a reality.

Medical Foundations

There is definitely a problem with the rising number of people who do not have health insurance. Some are unemployed. Some are working but their employer does not provide insurance while still others are working, do have insurance available but choose to gamble that they will save money and at the same time not become seriously ill. Some buy only catastrophic health insurance and choose to pay ongoing medical expenses out-of-pocket. Not having insurance is not the same as not having access to health care. There is a broad network of Federal, state, county, and municipal hospitals, virtually all of which have OP clinics as well as IP care. Many private hospitals, particularly teaching hospitals have a network of OP and IP services. Finally, there is a large and growing network of Free Clinics, staffed by residents of nearby hospitals, and both practicing physicians and retirees. A large cadre of volunteers, along with a small number of paid staff, make the clinic go. This treatment is certainly acceptable, but perhaps not the best we can offer. It tends to be a patchwork of care and therefore not very efficient. The only apparent alternative is some form of single-payer, Federal government program. From having served in three separate governmental health systems, and observing them closely, that is the last thing we want. The details of government-controlled medicine are discussed elsewhere (see "Government Medicine") but the reasons why this should not be a governmental system run by a huge governmental bureaucracy include: the lack of efficiency shown by any government bureaucracy, a frequent lack of being in touch with the clients it serves, a tendency to grow and grow and grow, and a sensitivity to pressure from politicians, lobbyists and self-interest groups, against which it would be difficult to stand up.

For purposes of discussion, let me propose an alternative scheme. This would address only the 20% of the population who are uninsured or under insured, not the 80% who do have some form of insurance. I would propose a series of foundations—private but quasi-public bodies with charitable tax exemptions. The quasi-public aspects would be appointment to the Board by the president of the United States or by the state governors, as there would be one national foundation and fifty state foundations. In time it may prove better to have a layer of regional foundations, and in more populous areas even county foundations, but for now let's explore foundations at two levels: federal and state.

The national (federal) foundation would not have the power to serve as a single-payer insurance company. Rather, it would serve as a resource to the state foundations. It would collect data and distribute them to the state foundations. These would include data about medical economics as well as medical and public health procedures. It would set up meetings for the state foundations. It would set up and distribute research funds for appropriate public health policies to the state foundations (who could farm out the research as it so chooses). Improvements in the provision of care could be made instantaneously available via the Internet.

The fifty state foundations would be similar in makeup to the national foundation, but it would be more involved in the day-to-day mechanics of the delivery of care to the uninsured. All would be hooked up to each other and the national foundation via the Internet for reaction to new advances in health care.

The staffing for the federal and state foundations would be similar. Each would by run by a Board of Governors, appointed by the President of the United States or by state governors. Some could be working people, but their time may be limited. Many could be active retirees—those who have held public office, who have been in public policy positions, who have been providers of health care, including practicing and non-practicing health care workers. A paid staff would carry out the policies and procedures of the Board, with emphasis on the leanness of the staff.

All of the above is well and good, but it would not function without funds—lots of funds. Here are some of the sources of the funds. All Medicaid funds could be given to the national foundation and then distributed to the state foundations. Sin taxes such as taxes on alcohol and cigarettes could go at least in part to the foundations, as could luxury taxes. A portion of the fines paid by drug dealers and drug users could go to the foundations, which would fund detoxification clinics. Patients could pay part of the costs of their care via a deductible and co-payment. The money received is not as important as the idea that one has a different attitude for something received for nothing to something for which one pays, at least in part. There could be a direct government subsidy and one could consider a national lottery, with all of the funds going to the foundations.

Finally, since these would be charitable organizations, contributions could be made to the foundations for the purpose of either operating budgets or endowment. Large corporations, large foundations as well as smaller personal foundations and individual gifts could supply significant funds in relatively short order.

Professional care could be provided in two ways. Either providers could receive payment for services rendered on a scale set by the foundation, or they could donate their services and receive a tax deduction. They could also receive the payment, donate the money to the endowment fund, and receive a tax deduction.

What are the advantages of such a structure? It would be a charitable organization, with a non-paid Board of Governors and a lean, paid staff. All would co-ordinate, one with the other, and all with the national foundation. As a charitable organization, it would be able to receive donations from a wide variety of sources. The money would not be taken from those with private insurance. Private practitioners (including retirees) would provide care. It would not be the large and ever growing bureaucracy that makes up a government program. Better co-ordination means better care. To me it is worth exploring.

Medical Gifts

An article appeared in the *New England Journal of Medicine (NEJM)* by a Dr. D. Waud, a professor of pharmacy at a New England medical school. In the article, he bitterly criticized the acceptance of gifts, by both practicing physicians and those in residency training programs from pharmaceutical companies, medical device companies, etc. The article appeared so unfair and so out of touch with reality that I feel compelled to reply.

Offering tree trips to faraway exotic places to physicians (and often their spouses) for the use of, or potential use of, a manufacturer's device or drug is a pernicious and corrupting process and one that should be curtailed. Offering "honoraria" (read "cash") to listen to a manufacturers's pitch is in the same category. However, when we enter pen and pencil land, as Dr. Waud[1] did in his commentary, the debate takes on the appearance of farce rather than serious discussion.

Dr. Waud is concerned that offering resident physicians pizza and beer for their medical rounds amounts to a bribe and should be shunned. It would be interesting to determine how many residents can be hopelessly corrupted by a single slice of pizza and how many require two or even three slices. What he apparently does not seem to understand is that there are usually several identical or similar products competing on the market rather than one single product, and the manufacturers of these products are competing for attention. Therefore, one company will offer pizza and beer, the second will offer coffee and doughnuts, the third, soft drinks, etc. Perhaps he could run a study (double-blinded, if possible) as to whether pizza or doughnuts have a more lasting corrupting effect on our young and impressionable residents. Of course, the whole problem could be obviated by having only one drug in each category—selected by people like himself, of course. This would have the unintended side effects of denying choice to our treating physicians as well as destroying our pharmaceutical industry, which is the wonder of the world and responsible for over 60% of new drugs entering the market on a worldwide basis.

There is nothing fundamentally wrong with enticing physicians to try a product—how else will they learn whether it is effective and useful in their own hands? But to go from this to the concept that physicians will continue to use a product ad infinitum, even when proven to be ineffective or less effective than a competing product, because they once accepted a free slice of pizza is to strain everyone's credulity.

I cannot speak for current residency practices, but I

can state the positive effects of having detailmen (of either gender) come to my office, in moderation of course. They offer a break in the routine. They are the purveyors of a little harmless local gossip ("Did you hear about the Dr. So-and-so?" "No, I hadn't heard."). I would not say they purvey pearls of wisdom as was mentioned in Dr. Waud's article, but rather semi-pearls of wisdom (or would it be pearls of semi-wisdom?) ("Do you know that some docs are using the product in this fashion or for this indication?" "No, I hadn't thought of it but it makes sense. Perhaps I will try it."). Finally, and by far the most important, they keep my drug cabinet stocked. I can then dispense medications to people I judge to be in need and I can have patients try a product in small amounts to see if it is going to be effective for them; if so, then a prescription can be written.

When we had graduated from medical school, all the seniors received an impressive medical bag. Unfortunately for the manufacturer who distributed the bag, I cannot remember for the life of me who gave it to us. Over the years I have received hundreds of pens and pencils, flashlights, letter openers, key rings, nail clippers, reflex hammers, pinwheels, anatomical models and charts, pocket- and wall-calendars and myriad other items, most lost and forgotten. My own personal favorite "bribe" is a scratch pad so I can write notes to my staff. If that makes me corrupt I will simply have to live with the disgrace. At meetings I have, courtesy of a pharmaceutical house, sipped coffee, and drunk sodas, nibbled on cookies and eaten doughnuts too numerous times to count. Unfortunately for all the manufacturers over all these years, I cannot remember who gave me what, and therefore I feel under no obligation to prescribe a particular product. These token gifts are simply a way of saying "thank you for taking the time to listen to me," and cannot be taken in the real world as an acceptance of a bribe.

Of course Dr. Waud is correct in stating that physicians can afford to go to meetings and pay their own way, but anyone who has been around for some time can see the astronomic rise in the costs of attending meetings. Some of that rise is self-inflicted and has been commented on elsewhere[2], but I for one am grateful that booksellers, pharmaceutical companies, equipment manufacturers, etc. are helping to hold meeting costs down to merely exorbitant and not bankrupting levels. This is *not* Dr. Waud's concern since presumably his university foots the bill for his attendance at a certain number of meetings. I also believe the *New England Journal of Medicine* should comment on what the costs to subscribers would be if advertising were removed from the journal. Again, this is probably not Dr. Waud's concern since his institution either pays for a certain number of his journals or gives him access via his department to those journals. Does Dr. Waud extend his preferred ban on advertising to Exhibit Halls at meetings, and if so, does he avoid, out of principle, meetings that do have Exhibit Halls? What does he think the cost of these things would be if exhibitors did not defray some of the expenses?

The relationship between physicians and those who manufacture products for our patients use is certainly a thorny one. There are clearly those selling techniques that are beyond the pale and should be banned. A large number are in a gray area and require some discrimination on the part of physicians. Some good guidelines for this are offered elsewhere in the *Journal*[3] and should be given wide circulation. It is very disturbing, however, when in the face of critical healthcare problems, the *Journal* gives repeated access to its pages for so-called problems as detailed by Dr. Waud and others. It is particularly galling to have such self-righteous comments come from academicians who do not share the burdens of earning a living by running a private practice. It is also surprising and disappointing that in all the discussions about controlling healthcare costs, there is no mention of controlling physician's costs—only the patient's costs. If there is guilt involved, or a need to feel good, the simple thing for Dr. Waud and others who feel as he does to do is not to accept anything at all from manufacturers. I believe what he has complained about is a non-problem, and in no way hampers physicians from providing the best care for their patients.

References

1. Waud, Dr. "Sounding Board." *New England Journal of Medicine* 1992: 327: 351–353.
2. Zohn, DA. "Compulsory Medical Education—The Downside." *VA Med Quarterly* 1990: Autumn.
3. Noble, RC. "Education or Promotion." *New England Journal of Medicine* 1992: 327: 363–364.

Medical-Legal Reform

Physicians have the dubious honor of being one of the first groups to suffer from a flood of liability suits. This is not in any way to deny that some physicians have done bad, negligent things and should be punished for those things. They should, and in some cases severely. However, bad outcomes are not the same as bad medical practice—there are hazards in medicine just as there are in life. One should work vigorously to reduce them, but perfection is a goal, not a reality.

It is said that the courts will sort out the truth but unfortunately that is not always the case. Juries are susceptible to emotion, and awards are presented because they believe that the insurance companies will pay. They do, but of course they raise their premiums to physicians who then strive mightily to pass these costs on to the patients. There is also a direct cost, as some physicians hire their own attorney since the attorney hired by the insurance company may not have the identical agenda as the physician himself. Even more important than the financial cost is the psychological cost, as physicians, whose role in life is helping people struggle with the claim that with intent they harmed a patient. This goes on for years and years as the case wends its way through the court system.

I do not think it is healthy for physicians to view their patients as potential legal threats rather than as sick people who come to them for help, but that is the reality. It is not healthy for physicians to practice defensive medicine, so that an attorney with complete 20/20 hindsight can claim that not ordering this or that procedure caused harm to his client. Finally, it is most unhealthy to see spawned from liability suits against physicians liability suits of every conceivable kind. In our current climate, no entity or individual is free from the pall hanging over them.

It is clear to me that medical-legal reform is essential and hopefully would lead to liability reform in other areas as well. Some of the ideas to be considered are the following: If something wrong has been done to an individual, he deserves to be compensated, but it should be through a no fault system rather than a tort system. The case should be adjudicated via arbitration or mediation rather than via the courts. If it must go to court, then, as in most countries, the loser pays the court fees. Lawyer fees should not be contingent on a percentage of the amount collected but on a multiple of their usual fees, plus of course reimbursement of expenses, the multiple to be set by a judge. The more difficult the case, the higher the multiple.

Physicians of course have their own role to play. There is a tremendous difference between a bad episode and a bad pattern. The latter calls for revocation of hospital staff membership and revocation of state licensure, while the former should raise a red flag and be further analyzed for future behavior modification on the part of the physician. Without pointing fingers, errors should be analyzed and procedures undertaken to minimize them, but it should be remembered that the system, as is true with all human systems, could never be perfect.

Working together, physicians and attorneys could fashion a system that addresses the needs of all parties—the patient/client, the physician and the lawyer. I won't hold my breath waiting for that to happen.

The Cost of Drugs

Currently there is a hue and cry about the high cost of drugs. It is perfectly true that some new, remarkable medicines carry a very high price tag. It is also true that they do remarkable things, treating and curing problems that were essentially untreatable and incurable only a short while ago. This has led to a significantly longer life span than was present only a generation or two ago. One might think that this would lead to eternal gratitude on the part of patients who have benefited from these wonders, but one would be quite wrong.

It is worthwhile remembering that the cost of drugs is only the latest in a long series of complaints about the cost of health care. Only a few years ago there was a hue and cry about the lack of catastrophic health care for the elderly. The problem was on its way to solution with a new benefit added to Medicare—for the additional cost of $75 per annum per person. This was vigorously opposed (the cost—not the benefit) by seniors and their lobby (AARP) and it was defeated. The next battle was fought over the provision of nursing home coverage, and then over home health services. All of these benefits are worthy, of course, but the benefit was requested at no increased cost to the individual. Somehow people are entitled and somehow the government will provide.

A good example of medical progress has been the treatment of hypertension (high blood pressure), a silent killer that may lead to heart disease, cerebrovascular disease, kidney disease and death. Only a couple of generations ago there was, if you can believe it, no treatment for the disease. There was emphasis on diet, particularly a low salt diet, and even what now seems to be the bizarre rice diet from Duke University, where individuals ate essentially nothing but rice. Then there were surgical treatments including the destruction of the sympathetic nervous chain in the belief that the sympathetic nervous system contributed to hypertension. It does, but unfortunately, its destruction by sympathectomy did not eliminate hypertension; it only produced its own medical complications. Now we have a whole series of drugs which simply and inexpensively control hypertension, with relatively few side effects. It is more a public health problem, getting people to have their blood pressure checked and then doing something about it if it is elevated. This did not come about by magic but by extensive and expensive research by the pharmaceutical companies.

One might ask why these new drugs are so expensive. In the past, drugs were not nearly so costly. They also were not nearly so effective. The explosion of knowledge, of technology and of know-how has led to truly remarkable advances in pharmaceutical therapy. These advances have started with huge sums devoted to research by the pharmaceutical industry—in the billions and billions of dollars. Every compound discovered is not a winner. Many, many fall by the wayside after early testing reveals that they are either ineffective or toxic. The few compounds that show promise are then subject to a multi-staged process of testing. Again, many compounds fail the test. After testing is completed, the approval process must be undertaken with the Food and Drug Administration (FDA). This is often a lengthy and expensive process with at least some of the costs borne by the pharmaceutical companies. If approval occurs, then the company must gear up for manufacture and marketing.

Once the drug is in wide use, problems may appear with some drugs, problems that were not recognized during the testing process as well as in the clinical trials which necessarily involve relatively limited numbers of individuals, and then it is necessary to withdraw the product from the market. If the new drug survives the above, it then faces an expiration of patent in only a relatively few years with the drug then manufactured as a generic product by another company at a far cheaper cost. The cost of bringing a successful new drug to market is in the hundreds of millions of dollars—for some compounds up to five hundred million dollars. It is therefore imperative that the few compounds which are successful pay for all those which were not, as well as provide the funds for additional research into new health problems. Do pharmaceutical companies make a nice profit? Of course they do. I say thank God for that, since I want them to do research on health problems which affect me (and you), and for which cures are not currently available.

Many people point out that drugs (the same drugs) are much cheaper in other countries (e.g. Canada) and some make a great show of going in groups to Canada where they purchase the drugs they want and need. Drugs are cheaper in Canada because the Canadian government subsidizes the cost of drugs. That is not the whole picture however, since health care costs are not totally elastic. If drugs are cheaper, then the health care money must come from somewhere else. This results in delays in improving technology, delays in diagnostic testing and delays in elective therapy. Indeed, these delays (really rationing) has resulted in many Canadians paying out of pocket to get their testing and treatment—in the U.S. Indeed, health care facilities in northern American cities from Seattle to Boston have benefited markedly from an influx of Canadian patients.

There is also another aspect to the high cost of drugs, and that is that one must look at the total picture of health care costs. Treating a patient effectively with a drug, on an outpatient basis, no matter how expensive the drug, is far cheaper than bringing the patient into the hospital. Prevention of a problem is always far cheaper than treatment of a problem. The patient, however, does not look at the totality of health care costs, but only how much is paid out of pocket. Since most inpatient costs are covered by insurance, the patient does not see the real cost of such a stay.

There is a peculiar attitude of people towards products that they need and on which they are dependent. These include energy products (oil and gas), utility products (electricity), transportation products (airline tickets) and of course health care products (pharmaceuticals, medical devices, health care services). When these prices rise, as they periodically do, people scream that they are being gouged, that the industries are robber barons, they should be controlled by the government, etc. However, most of these industries are cyclical. When the inevitable downturn comes, there is never, and I mean never, a suggestion that people should pay more to help these industries out. Complete and total silence.

An even more difficult problem has been the AIDS epidemic in Africa and parts of Asia. It is undoubtedly a tragedy of the highest order. The solution proposed is that, in spite of patent protection for the pharmaceutical companies who manufacture the anti-AIDS drugs, generic drugs be produced by other manufacturers for distribution to the unfortunates, at a much cheaper price. The impulse is understandable, but there are many problems with the solution. On a practical level, far more than the presence of drugs is necessary to curb the outbreak. A whole infrastructure must be put in place. This would include adequate hospitals and clinics, well trained professionals, a complete public health structure including lesser trained individuals who can visit the victims and be sure that they are complying with the program, appropriate education for both children and adults, and of course the assuming of personal responsibility by the citizens. Virtually none of that exists in most of the countries where the epidemic is raging.

Further, the responsibility should not be primarily on the shoulders of the manufacturers, but on the governments of the countries where the epidemic is present. I know that people will claim that these governments are impoverished and therefore cannot do anything, but decades of corruption, greed, incompetence and perennial warfare leading to the impoverishment do not excuse these governments from their responsibility of providing for the basic needs of their people. Also the wealthier nations of the world. Also the international organizations of the world, such as the United Nations. Also the international aid organizations. Instead, they all lean on the manufacturers to give up their precious patents.

Now of course the manufacturers should, and indeed are, doing their part. They are however private for-profit organizations with responsibilities to their risk takers (lenders—banks and bond holders, stockholders) as well as their stakeholders (workers, communities where they have manufacturing plants). An even larger problem is the violation of patents. If it is done for one group for one disease it for sure will be asked to do it for others—and that spells the end of these companies for obvious reasons. An extraordinarily difficult problem which cannot be solved by mindless calls for only one party to make sacrifices—and the wrong party at that.

Nevertheless, after all is said and done, modern, effective drug therapy can be very expensive. Most people can bear the cost, although of course they do not like it, any more than they like any out of pocket health costs. Some way will have to be found to subsidize these drug costs for the very poor, but the most likely outcome of that action is that something else will be sacrificed. In a way, drugs costs are a metaphor for all of modern health care. Remarkable medical advances have improved and lengthened the lives of millions, but these advances do not come without cost. Trade-offs are necessary. To me, one obvious trade-off is to lengthen the time of patent protection for the manufacturers, so they have more time to recoup their costs and indeed make a profit. These are not public utilities and I see nothing wrong or evil in making a profit. I'm sure that other trade-offs can be thought of, but I strongly suspect that people want something for nothing.

The Interrelationship of Health Care and Social Issues

The *Journal of the American Medical Association* (JAMA) has broken new ground with publication of the thoughtful article by Shoemaker et al[1]. This article clearly points out the close interrelationship between medicine and the nation's social problems. It is these social problems which are markedly escalating the costs of medicine as much as any of the other factors mentioned in any discussion of needed health care reforms. On top of that it is probably not too much to say that these social problems have produced a crisis in this country which is as much of a threat to our survival and well being as was World War II.

Since this is a national problem, all of us should be concerned about it. Questions of motivation by love or hate, prejudice or tolerance are really irrelevant at this time—the only thing necessary is that various solutions be posed, a consensus be built and action taken—all better sooner than later.

Whether right or wrong, I would like to outline problems and propose solutions from a different perspective than Shoemaker et al and hope that it will stimulate debate.

Perceptions

The social problems tearing apart our society, most particularly drugs and violence, have not been discussed openly and honestly in our society in spite of their seriousness. These problems did not start this year or last but have been developing over the past quarter century or more. As painful as it is to say, the black community has shut off debate by calling those whites that have tried to talk about the problems racists. Since initially the problems were limited to the inner city and since nobody enjoyed being called a racist, whites held their tongues. This was obviously a mistake since it was impossible for such problems to be limited to the inner city and by now they have spread far beyond the inner city confines. A segment of white opinion also has contributed to the silence. By claiming that legitimate criticism was in effect blaming the victim, and pointing to past injustices as a reason (in reality an excuse) for anti-social behavior has exacerbated rather than reduced the problem. The triad of guns, drugs and violence represents one of the major health problems of our time. Getting control of this problem, even lessening if not abolishing it, should contribute in a major way to reducing health care costs, as well as improving the quality of health care, as the graphic descriptions of Shoemaker et al of health care in an inner city hospital attest.

It is perfectly obvious to all but the most rabid that further gun control is necessary. There is no place in civilian society for automatic weapons—not for sport and not for self-protection. Since we register our cars and pets, and license and credential everyone concerned with public safety it is difficult to know why in a modern society the same should not be true of guns. This of course does not in any way imply that individuals should not own guns. The real problem however, and one that goes hand and hand with trying to get some control over guns, is what to do with those who violate the law. What exactly do we do with juveniles who carry guns on the street or in the school and what do we do with criminals who carry guns while committing a felony, or actually use a gun in the course of committing a felony? How do we deal with people who fail to register their guns? A decision on how to handle these problems goes hand in hand with further gun control.

Drugs are the second leg of this triad. Officials from Colombia and other countries have begged us to cut down on usage but the major effects have centered on interdiction and public health measures for known addicts. There really should be no debate about treatment versus interdiction since both are important but neither in themselves stands much chance of success in resolving the problem. One approach has been the effort to legalize illicit drugs, which has drawn support from people on all sides of the political spectrum. After one gets beyond the philosophizing and intellectualizing and into the details, it becomes clear why it is an idea that cannot work.[2] Asking a few simple questions should explain why. Exactly how will drugs be kept out of the hands of juveniles when they find it so extraordinarily easy to obtain alcohol and tobacco? Will all drugs be available for sale or will some be left in the hands of drugs dealers? Are we prepared to enter into a price war with dealers who will not so easily give up their multi-billion-dollar industry? What will happen to our so carefully constructed control of legal drugs if the government is busy dispensing currently illegal drugs to any comers? There are many other arguments which can be made against legalization but by far the most important of them is the moral one. If we give tacit approval to the use of illicit drugs, and are unable to find the will to combat the problem, how will we justify our fight on any one of the many other social issues that are plaguing us?

It seems to me that the only way to attack the problem is to declare war on the users who for the most part come from the middle class. It is not necessary to build more courts and jails for them. Exorbitant fines and public humiliation (name and picture printed in the paper, in the case of teenagers appearance with their parents at a school assembly) would appear to be appropriate avenues of approach. Perhaps the removal of driving privileges might also be appropriate. The problem for inner city users is much more difficult since the above punishments are not really applicable. Here the necessity of treatment and education would be paramount as well as more long-term solutions for inner city problems (see below).

This approach obviously raises civil liberties issues and one should be prepared for a major backlash from civil libertarians. Civil liberties gained over the course of centuries at no small cost are not easily given up. Nevertheless we should remember that these liberties are not absolute. They are given by man and can be taken away by man at appropriate times and for appropriate reasons. We fully recognize that in wartime we have to give up certain freedoms for our mutual benefit. Are we now not at war?

When the crisis has passed the American people in their wisdom will undoubtedly restore them to their prewar state. Finally we should realize that we are seeing major violations of the civil liberties of the innocent. Our most basic freedom to be safe in our houses, cars and on the streets are regularly being violated while the criminals roam free. This is not always the way it was and we must restore society to the way it was.

Violence is the third leg of the triad. One explanation is that this is the result of human misery. Remove the misery and the violence will disappear. This explanation forgets that during the Great Depression there was even more human misery than there is now—it enveloped the entire country and not just portions of it—and yet we had nowhere near the violence directed against individuals that we have now. Clearly other factors are at work. To put a name on it, we are being preyed upon by amoral predators. Every day the papers and television bring us new stories that exceed what we had considered to be the outer limits of deviant behavior. Their frequency numbs us and paralyzes us. How such behaviors came about is a subject for a national debate—but at the end of the debate a consensus should be reached and a course of action prescribed.

Long-Term Solutions

Changing our perceptions to deal with the self-evident reality of social disarray and chaos in the inner cities, curbing of illegal gun use and the crime and violence that go along with it and controlling drug usage are all short term solutions to staunch the flow but are no substitute for long term solutions. Gun control and violence control as proposed by Shoemaker et al are certainly worthwhile but can hardly be the entire solution.

55

Proposal

Recommendations for better education, better jobs and better health are often recited like mantras as a cure for the problems of the inner cities. How can anyone be against any of them? If large-scale resources are to be devoted to these efforts and if they will produce the desired goals, then we should of course all be prepared to make a sacrifice for the common good. As with drug legalization, discussion seldom progresses beyond the superficial and philosophical. What proponents need to say is that x amount of dollars will produce y results in z years. Failure to meet those goals represents failure of the program(s) and should be terminated. I personally have great doubts that such programs can work. Take for example a job for an inner city male age eighteen to twenty-five. In all likelihood, he is a high school dropout and a functional illiterate. He possesses no specialized skills—at least for legitimate work. He is not used to discipline and would bristle at having to take orders, let alone appear on time regularly. Being unemployed, he is used to sleeping all day and roaming the streets at night. This is not being said in criticism—merely to state reality and to point out the difficulty of the problem. Clearly a different approach is needed.

Such a change would take place if the black community would take primary responsibility for rebuilding the social structure that disappeared when middle class blacks left the inner cities for a better life in the more affluent sections of the city or the suburbs. They of course should not have sole responsibility and there undoubtedly will be help from the larger society but I have yet to see mentioned anywhere that the black community bears primary responsibility for the resocialization of the inner cities. Indeed, after the Los Angeles riots, condemnation of the various government entities as well as segments of the white community (e.g., the entertainment industry) for not doing more to rebuild South Central Los Angeles was made, but no mention of what plans the black community had for its own rebirth was forthcoming.

For those who claim that the black community does not have the resources to redevelop the riot torn area, consider this scenario. There are two major league franchises in football, basketball and baseball in the greater LA area.* Assuming that there are a total of two hundred players, that half are black and that they earn an average of one million dollars each, that represents one hundred million dollars per year of earned income. Make the same assumption for the entertainment industry and you have another one hundred million dollars of earned income. Assume that there are one thousand professionals, businessmen, executives and entrepreneurs earning $250,000 each and that represents another two hundred and fifty million dollars. Finally, assume there are ten thousand petit bourgeoisie—small businessmen, young professionals, young executives etc. earning $75,000 each and you have another 750 million dollars of earned income. Add them all together and you have 1.2 billion of earned income coming from just one percent of the estimated one million black residents of greater Los Angeles. If 10%, or one hundred million dollars, were invested for profit in South Central, there would be in ten years time one billion dollars invested. That would be exclusive of reinvestment of profit, charitable donations, investment from the white community and from government. Larger investors

_____
* Since this was written, the two professional football teams have left the Los Angeles area but the principle remains intact.

could invest in individual projects while smaller invest-ors could band together and hire a project manager to select projects and oversee them. Such projects could in-clude neighborhood banks, home improvement compa-nies, franchises, small businesses, artisan and craft cooperatives and a whole host of other projects. Investing for profit would insure some degree of supervision by the investors and as they see fit, investment in both human and physical infrastructure. There should follow a grad-ual return of social norms of behavior as the younger children mature in a more structured environment. As a bonus, a sense of pride and accomplishment should spread throughout the entire black community and they would see they are quite capable of doing something pro-ductive without the corrosive effect of the government doing it for them. If successful, it could be replicated throughout the country.

Conclusion

There is little question that the social fabric of this country is being strained to the breaking point today. If we fail to take effective and appropriate action now, who knows what tomorrow will bring? As a first stage, control of violent acts against individuals must be undertaken, either by what has been outlined above or whatever works. There is no liberty and no freedom if we are not safe in our person. The second stage is the long-term solu-tion. Here changes in perceptions amongst all of us must take place. The return of the black community to the role of primary responsibility for initiating actions is a prerequisite. This should lead to a reestablishment of a more normal social order and a sense of community in the inner city. Finally, we in the larger community must all participate, but our role should clearly be a secondary one.

Hopefully, success here can lead to significant reductions in health care expenses. Emergency rooms would be treating primarily medical emergencies and not social emergencies—gun shot wounds, drug overdoses, violence-related injuries. Improved employment would lead to individuals having health insurance, putting less of a strain on the system. As employment rises, hopefully people will begin to practice preventive care and the severity of many illnesses as well as their duration can be lessened. It cannot be said that this alone will solve the tremendous health care costs but it can go a long way to help.

References

1. "Urban violence in Los Angeles in the aftemath of the riots." Shoemaker, W.C., James, C.B., King, L.M., Hardin, E., Ordog, G.J. JAMA Vol. 270 #23:2833 1993.
2. Zohn, D.A. "Legalizing Drugs: a few simple questions" *Virginia Medical* Vol. 117 #6:250 1990.

Clinical Observations

(Materia Miscellanea Medica)

Brief Random Thoughts

"Me-Too" Drugs

Periodically there is an outcry, usually from non-practicing physicians, that pharmaceutical companies make too many "me-too" drugs—that is, drugs which are identical or very similar in their chemical nature. To me that has always been a very strange complaint.

Pharmaceutical companies are private companies in business to earn money for their shareholders. If they thought they would not make a return on their investment, they would not produce the drug. It cannot be said that the money would be better spent on R&D (Research and Development) since the companies already spend enormous amounts on that—an amount as high if not higher than any other industry. Further, the presence of several drugs of identical or similar nature provides the consumer and the prescribing physician with a choice, and holds down costs that might be much higher if there were a monopoly on that particular class of drugs. Isn't that highly desirable?

In addition, there are often many valuable features that differentiate one drug from the others. One claims (and according to the FDA—the Food and Drug Administration—you can only claim what can be demonstrated to be true) that it has an earlier onset of action, so that relief comes sooner. Another has a longer duration of action, permitting fewer doses per day. This produces better compliance on the part of the patient since they are less likely to omit a dose. Still another claims to have fewer side effects that are known to occur with this class of drug, while another claims to be less expensive. Finally there is the idiosyncratic effect—one drug produces no favorable response in a patient while another similar drug produces the expected effect. The reverse may be true for the next patient. Why this is so is not at all clear but any practicing physician can tell you that it is not at all uncommon. If we had a central planning agency we would have just one drug in each category. If it works, fine, and if it doesn't, that's just tough.

Physician Advertising

It has been going on for more than a decade so I should be used to it by now, but I am constantly irritated on seeing advertising by physicians. In newspapers, magazines, on radio and television, etc. Usually there is a made-up name for the group doing the advertising (and all except plastic surgeons advertise as a group so you do not know whom the individuals are—you only know the product: eye care, skin care, pain relief, etc.). One can say *caveat emptor*—let the buyer beware—but it seems strange to entrust your health to someone whom you only know because of a catchy jingle, testimonials or just a strong sales pitch.

To me it sets up a dilemma and acts against their own best interests: Physicians wish to be seen and

61

treated like professionals but they behave, with their advertising, as tradesmen. I know other professionals such as lawyers advertise extensively, but that is exactly why physicians should not advertise.

Patient Responsibility

There is no doubt that medical care in this country is expensive, for reasons outlined elsewhere. Whether the costs are excessive or appropriate for the needs of a modern, wealthy society with a desire for the best care possible is a topic for another time and place. What is not thought about is the role of patient responsibility in driving up the costs of medical care.

Patient responsibility involves an avoidance of certain social conditions that add not only to societal costs but health costs as well. Smoking, drinking to excess, driving under the influence of alcohol, use of non-legal drugs, careless driving which leads to accidents and injury, violent acts which lead to personal injury and many other actions lead to health care costs above and beyond the costs of insurance coverage. Even problems which are covered by insurance lead to ever rising premiums to cover the costs—money that could be put to good use elsewhere. It is always amazing to me that people demand freedom to do whatever they wish and then complain bitterly about the high cost of health care, which in large part arises from avoidable actions. They also appear to feel that the health problems that result from their behavior somehow just come upon them spontaneously, and their actions had nothing to do with these problems.

It is not just avoidable social actions that produce health problems, and therefore health costs. It is actions within the physician's office which lead to additional costs. Failure to follow prescribed treatment programs, failure to keep appointments so their progress can be monitored, failure to check symptoms early, continued doctor shopping until one gets the answer one wants all may lead to a prolongation of the illness and hence a rise in costs. There is certainly no guarantee that one will get well if all of the above are not factors in the treatment program, but it is likely that they will do nothing to aid in rapid recovery.

Animal Rights Activists

Animal rights activists have gotten some things right. Some research labs kept animals in sub-standard conditions. Some researchers sacrificed animals to obtain information that could be obtained by other means, such as computers. Some research labs may have been indifferent to animal suffering. When I say some, I mean a very small number. Most labs have tried their best to run a humane lab. Most researchers get little personal pleasure from sacrificing animals to obtain vital health information. Animal rights activists portray research scientists as cruel, sadistic fiends, which is so ludicrous and far from the truth that they do nothing but discredit themselves.

Virtually every advance in modern medicine has been the result of animal research. Matters of efficacy and safety are often only obtained by animal testing. Surgeons hone their skills in the dog labs. Can anyone seriously think that medical advances, potentially harmful to humans (e.g. drug effects) as well as medical skills should not be tested and honed before being tried on humans? Apparently there are some true believers that do think like that—and they are impervious to facts and logic. They also arrogate to themselves the right to kill or destroy, but cannot even grant to their opponents the sincerity of their beliefs.

Solutions to the problem are in sight. The prohibitive costs of animal labs will force more and more computer simulations. They (animal experiments) will not be eliminated completely, but they will be reduced. Other solutions come to mind. Each animal rights activist should wear a tag which categorically rejects any treatment, medical or surgical, which has animal experimentation in its background. Of course that eliminates virtually all of modern medicine, but that should be the price one pays for one's beliefs. It seems more than slightly hypocritical to at the same time attack animal experimentation and yet benefit from it when the need arises. A second solution to avoid animal experimentation is for the protesters to offer themselves as subjects for the medical experiments needed before a new treatment can be brought to market. How noble that would be. Unfortunately it is easier to rant and rave than to approach a problem from the point of view of reality.

GPs

The most striking example to me of the changed relationship between physician and patient comes about during the Christmas season. In the earlier days of my practice, I used to get gifts—gobs of gifts—from my patients. I used to call them gifts from GPs (Grateful Patients). They came in all forms but most often were baskets of fruit, cheeses or chocolates, as well as bottles of liquor. Often they were homemade, consisting of jams or preserves, knitted items and the like. They were accompanied by notes wishing me and mine a happy holiday season and indicating how grateful they were for the care they had received. I felt so proud that I had been

64

able to help someone and grateful to them that they recognized that. Respect was evident and what I was doing truly seemed worthwhile.

Towards the end of my medical career, all of that changed. I would still get the occasional gift but certainly nothing like what it had been. I did not need what the patients brought and my ego was not damaged because they no longer brought gifts. Further, I provided the same service in the same fashion as before, but I was truly saddened by the changed relationship. Whereas before it appeared to be a personal as well as a professional relationship, now it was impersonal and businesslike. I provided a service for which they paid (sometimes) and nothing further was required. I feel something has been lost.

Medical Dicta (Aphorisms)

Health care costs are of concern only to the healthy.
When ill, only the best will do—and damn the costs.
Everyone wants the best health care available—they just don't want to pay for it.
Living is hazardous to your health.
Thoughts on retirement:

- How do you like retirement? Beats working.
- What do you do with your time? Go to the doctor's office.
- Do you travel? Back and forth to the doctor's office.

The healthy make the rules for the ill.
When you are well, your only concern is cost. When you are ill, your only concern is getting well.
When you are well, your insurance policy is a burden; when ill, it is a lifeline.

65

Insurance companies try to decrease expenses and increase profits. Physicians try to help patients. They are fundamentally incompatible.

Physicians cannot promise a cure—only a best effort.

Medical care is a bottomless pit.

Old medical dictum: Piss and puss must come out.

In pre-antibiotic era, Salvarsan (a mercury product) was the only treatment for syphilis. One night with Venus; six months with Mercury.

Old Habits Die Hard

I was appointed Chief of Service at a large municipal hospital, a part of an even larger Department of Health. Although I had more on my plate than I could manage, I was informed that in addition to my duties at the hospital, I was to be in charge of all facilities having to do with my specialty: rehabilitation. From a bureaucratic standpoint (the only one that counted to the Department of Health bureaucrats), it made sense—one could easily see the Table of Organization boxes that bureaucrats love to play with. From my point of view, it made no sense whatsoever. I was short staffed already, and these other entities were functioning adequately. I had no desire or time to be drawn into endless turf battles, but willy nilly I was.

One of the facilities I was to "supervise" was a former tuberculosis (TB) sanitarium, staffed by internists and pulmonologists, most of whom had been in the field of treatment of TB for many years. When drug therapy brought about what was thought to be the end of TB as a major health problem, it was decided to close down the sanitarium and re-open it as a rehabilitation facility. The medical staff, however, remained the same.

In the course of my duties, I attended grand rounds at the newly established rehabilitation facility. A patient who had had a stroke was presented. After a cursory discussion of the diagnosis and treatment of stroke, they got down to the meat of the issue—the chest x-ray. Discussion of this took up most of the time for the grand rounds. To prevent myself from laughing out loud, I left the meeting before its conclusion. It was clear that you could recycle the hospital but not necessarily the M.D.s. Old habits die hard.

Pain Clinics

As my practice evolved, I became primarily involved in the treatment of patients with pain problems—usually chronic pain problems. I attended (and organized) many pain clinics, and of course kept up with other pain clinics in the area, and even on a national basis. It was a source of silent amusement to me to see and hear how the clinics took on the coloration of the specialty of the people running the clinic.

For example, if the clinic were run by a psychiatrist, the patients would gather around in a group and discuss the psychological problems related to the chronic pain. If run by a surgeon, (orthopedist or neurosurgeon) the emphasis was on performing surgery to relieve the pain. If run by an anesthesiologist, the emphasis was on performing various nerve blocks. If run by a neurologist or internist, the emphasis was on prescribing medications, while if by a physiatrist, the emphasis was on treatment with various physical therapeutic measures. To overcome that, I established a multispecialty pain clinic, but that did not solve the problem. The observations by the various specialists were simply a reiteration of their solution based upon the treatment measures that they had been trained to provide. The discussions were often very heated because of that. Only a very few were able to step back and think out of the box.

Physicians as Social Workers

Part of the job of being a physician is learning effective counseling and to a degree most physicians do it. But physicians are not social workers nor do they have as their primary impulse the desire to be social workers. They are nevertheless asked to have the knowledge and skills of a social worker. They are also asked to be fully aware of the lay literature on non-prescription and prescription medicines, and to be intimately acquainted with the myriad alternative medicine treatments. When a discussion group I overheard talked about a lack of knowledge among physicians about alternative medicines and medical cares, they had a simple solution—teach it in medical school! They did not specify which courses should be displaced to make way for the new course—after all, it is generally recognized that the plate of courses the medical student consumes is more than slightly full. The public is constantly adding to the list items at which the physicians must be proficient: computers, business and finance, etc. It is often forgotten that some physicians just wish to provide medical care.

Closed Minds

It was certainly not true of all physicians, perhaps not even the majority of physicians, but I did notice throughout my career a tendency among some physicians to have absolutely closed minds about certain new things. I was particularly struck by this phenomenon because a series of happenstances led me to use on my patients (effectively I might say) a number of techniques which were not at the time in general usage nor did they have wide acceptance.

In general terms, I think physicians are absolutely right to be skeptical about new things. I personally preferred to be one of the later users of new medications rather than one of the first. Let someone else discover the previously unknown side effects and deal with them. Further, these techniques, procedures, medications, etc. should be proven before being used, employing scientific techniques of appropriately blinded studies to reach a conclusion about effectiveness. However, some clinical techniques are not readily amenable to scientific study and we should not completely abandon sound empirical observation as a means of employing effective treatment. We should remember that aspirin was used effectively for nearly one hundred years before we discovered the nature of its mechanism of action. Its usage was based on sound observation of its effectiveness.

However, being skeptical and being conservative is not the same thing as having a completely closed mind. I obtained the impression from the words and actions of some physicians that if something wasn't taught in medical school or in a residency program, it wasn't worth knowing. This is an historic attitude that for example led to the ostracism of Dr. Semmelweis of Vienna, Austria, because he saw the relationship between cleanliness of the hands and the transmission of puerperal fever to women giving birth. It was the habit of physicians in the mid-nineteenth century to come directly to the delivery room from the dissecting room without the intermediary step of careful hand washing. Dr. Semmelweis was able to drastically reduce puerperal fever by the employment of that intermediary step-and was roundly denounced by his colleagues for that. There are many examples in history of similar advances being greeted with the same attitude.

Of course physicians are constantly bombarded by patients, manufacturers and others to employ new procedure treatments, medications, etc. There are literally hundreds and hundreds of these techniques that are generically called alternative medicine. Most are completely unproven, touted by people without a scientific background and are backed up only by testimonials, a notoriously unreliable and often dishonest technique. Further, physicians are well aware of the placebo effect in which the patient apparently obtains benefit simply from the taking of a sham pill or performing a sham procedure, indicating how important the mind is in the expression of pain. Many years ago a procedure was done which certainly could not be performed today. For the treatment of angina (and at that time there were no effective treatments for angina), a scar was made on the chest but nothing further was done. Believing that a helpful procedure had been performed, a number of patients reported a reduction in their angina. I have seen figures varying from 33 to 50 percent improvement simply from the placebo effect. Often, of course, the relief does not last but there is no question that the placebo effect is a powerful one. The National Institutes of Health now has a Division of Alternative Medicine which will explore with the best scientific methods possible the benefits, or lack thereof, of various alternative medicine techniques. I strongly suspect that most will be of no benefit or will simply show the placebo effect, but perhaps there will be some pearls which will prove to be of real benefit to patients.

As noted above, I was conventionally trained in medical school and in residency training and employed primarily conventional techniques on my patients. In addition, I also used other techniques that had not gained general acceptance by the medical community. These techniques were not based on testimonials or other flimsy evidence but were reported by well-trained physicians, discussed at appropriate professional meetings and published in established journals. Often I would provide relief to patients who had not benefited from conventional techniques. No matter how often that happened, the reaction from some physicians was always the same—either there was really nothing there in the first place or it was something which would have gotten better by itself. Why it didn't get better under their care was never explained. What bothered me as much as the closed minds was the complete lack of intellectual curiosity. I can never recall these physicians saying that they would like to see what was done and perhaps try it themselves. Unfortunately, as I have shown, this is an historic attitude that has infected members of the medical community for centuries.

Doctor Talk

Over the years, I observed that when a group of physicians got together they would discuss many things, as would any other group of people: family, politics, sports, weather, and professional gossip. The one thing, however, which really animated them was interesting and difficult medical cases. There was even a name for these cases—fascinomas. They would report the case to the listeners, describe how they tried or succeeded in solving the problem, solicited advice when necessary (this also has a name—curbside consultations) and just took great pleasure in the discussion. This was true not only of the younger and newer physicians but more senior physicians as well. I would often see their eyes light up as they described a difficult or interesting medical problem. When I was a house officer and even later when I was a young attending physician they would drag me to the bedside to show me the problem at first hand, even if they had no obligation to do so. The picking up of an obscure diagnosis was a source of great pride to all.

All of this started to change in the late seventies and the early eighties when the problems relating to physician liability started to gain prominence. The nature of physician discussions changed radically. All that one heard were discussions about liability: gossip about who had been sued and for what cause, what insurance company to go with, what to do about limiting liability, etc. Staff meetings, medical society meetings, professional society meetings all began to be dominated by the topic of liability and how to deal with it. Some entrepreneurs made a great deal of money by giving courses on how to deal with the problem. Medical societies even formed support groups to help physicians who were sued to deal with the problem.

By the late eighties and the nineties, the discussions shifted to woes with insurance companies—the games they played to delay or avoid payment, the advent of HMOs, PPOs and the like, the pros and cons of capitation, and medical woes in general. The physician went from being considered a highly respected professional to, in the minds of much of the public, a money grubbing businessman who had to be put in his place, until of course, one desperately needed his services.

Toward the end of my career, I would sit through all kinds of meetings and never once heard the previously-heard stories of interesting cases. How terribly sad for everyone.

Fairness

Over and over, I hear people insisting that fairness should be the criteria for medical care, by which I presume the speaker means that everyone should get equal care. Forget that life itself is unfair. Forget that the equality of physicians (and of the hospitals and support staff) can vary greatly. Forget that some people are ill-fed, ill-housed and ill-clothed. We as a society will do what we can to help the least fortunate, but there will never be full equality in those areas—nor should there be. Forget all of the above and people still want perfect equality.

Here is why there can never be perfect equality. Health care is based on three parameters: quality, access, and cost. Each is essential to provide health care. It is certainly possible for a legislature and a bureaucracy to insist on equal access but how does one legislate quality of care and costs? Well, you might say, have the Federal government control all health care. Without going into detail, that battle was fought in the early nineties over the ill-fated Clinton health care reform act, and lost decisively.

The choice of people who cannot afford insurance is not health care or no health care at all. We have in place a very elaborate system of care for such people. The Federal government has in place an elaborate system of hospitals and clinics for those eligible (veterans, merchant seamen, Native Americans, the Medicaid program for the indigent), while states have in place a system of mental institutions and mental health care clinics. Cities and counties have municipal general care hospitals and clinics while many large teaching private hospitals have wards for indigent patients. In some cases, because of the interest and enthusiasm of the house staffs (residents, interns and students) care is better than in private care. Admittedly in some cases it is clearly worse, but the point is, that with or without insurance, everyone receives at least the fundamentals of health care. There is also a large and growing network of Free Clinics, staffed by physician and non-physician volunteers and including many retired physicians who volunteer their services.

I am certainly in favor of providing the best care possible for as many people as possible, but not at the price of huge tax increases and a smothering and all-consuming bureaucracy.

Physician's Income

One of the recurring myths floating around is that physicians are greedy, vastly overpaid and they don't deserve what they get. It is perfectly true that there are some "big hitters" out there, who, because of their specialty, their additional training or their own abilities, earn large sums of money—up to and including seven figures. A more accurate figure is the physician's median income in which half earn more and half earn less than the median (it is obviously less than the average, which is skewed by the earnings of a few "big hitters"). This currently is approximately $160,000. Not too shabby but one should examine this further. First, it is predicated on a sixty-hour workweek, which lowers the income significantly. A decade or more of hard work and stress goes into the making of a physician, including formal schooling and postgraduate training (internship, residency, fellowship), all after college. Shouldn't there be some assigned value to that? Patient care is not limited by the hour of the day, weekends, holidays, etc. Shouldn't there be some value assigned to that? Finally, decisions regarding the health and even the life of an individual patient are constantly required to be made. Shouldn't there be some value assigned to that? Apparently not. Some people want nothing but the best quality of care available—cheap.

At one time, irritated by the constant complaints about physician incomes, I drew up a table comparing physician incomes with those of people who are considered to be vastly underpaid: college professors. If one looked at income for just one year, it was obvious that physicians earned much much more than college professors—no comparison at all. However, if one looked at the complete picture over forty to fifty years, the picture was quite different. After a year spent earning a masters degree, a college professor was employable and earned a living teaching in his field while working on his doctorate. A physician on the other hand, had to pay tuition while attending school. The workload was so onerous that there was no time whatsoever to earn a living while attending school. Most physicians graduated with a very hefty debt from his or her schooling, a debt that usually took several decades to pay off. During postgraduate training, a resident or fellow was paid only nominally, while working extraordinarily long and hard. To give one an idea of this, there are repeated efforts to limit the workload to eighty hours per week, but this is apparently frequently violated because of the necessity to provide ongoing care.

Once in practice, life is easier, even with the necessity of repaying debt, but it is scarcely a bed of roses. As I have mentioned, the average workload is sixty hours per week. Compare that to the twenty hours for a college professor. The average vacation time is six weeks per year. Compare that to the twenty weeks for a college professor. Somehow one has to factor in the working on nights, weekends and holidays. One has to factor in the constant awakening by calls from the hospital or patient when one is on call. Even when off, it is frequently necessary to field phone calls and to go into the hospital to complete records and perform other paperwork.

On the other side of the ledger, a college professor is entitled to a large menu of perks. Benefits like health insurance and payments into a retirement fund are provided. A sabbatical year comes about several times during a career. Yes, the time is often spent in doing research in one's field, but who wouldn't like the luxury of studying or doing research in one's field while being paid for it? College tuition for one's children can amount to a huge sum of money that is paid for by the employing college.

When the ledger is added up, and due attention is paid to the intangibles such as work stress, hours worked, sacrifice of nights, weekends and holidays, sacrifice of family life, etc., there is really not a great deal of difference between the incomes of the two groups. I do not wish to change places, nor do I minimize the good work performed by our college faculties in educating our young. I am merely pointing out that the apparent huge difference in incomes is not huge at all when properly calculated.

For the first half of the twentieth century, the majority of physicians did extremely hard and demanding work for very little pay. What changed? Medicine changed. As knowledge grew, specialization grew, and specialists, appropriately, charged more for their services. The length of training in residencies (earlier there were essentially no residencies, just a year of internship and then on to practice; those who wished additional training apprenticed themselves to someone or worked in clinics, or taught themselves) continued to expand, and greater compensation for greater training was sought. Technology exploded. Most of the larger, more complex technologies were done in the hospital, but many more procedures could be done in the office of the physician. It is probably not understood that if a physician just worked in his office and just saw patients, he would not be able to pay the rent. The diagnostic and therapeutic measures performed in the office are not only essential to the care of the patient but are the profit margin. It is also probably not understood that although a physician is paid for his services when he sees a patient in the hospital, he receives none of the income if he orders procedures to be performed, unless he does them himself. The income goes to the hospital, and then is disbursed to the various hospital based physicians such as radiologists and anesthesiologists. Travel time, medical record time, meeting time, etc. all are necessary, but inhibit the physician's ability to earn a living.

Insurance also changed. At the beginning of the second half of the twentieth century, health insurance coverage for workers became the norm. Medicare kicked in a decade or so later. Although physicians (correctly) opposed it as a progressively more expensive proposition, it proved to be a financial boon to them, as the aging population grew vastly. Before, some mechanisms used for the elderly (and indeed others without insurance) were barter, fee reduction (or no fee) and under the table transactions. This was no longer necessary when a third party was the payer, and most people, if working, had reasonably good insurance coverage.

To me, considering the above, physician incomes, particularly compared with other elements in society and based upon their awesome responsibilities, are in fact relatively modest. Finally, what is not considered is that if physicians were interested primarily in money, they would never sacrifice a decade of their life, take on huge school debts, and enter a very difficult lifestyle. They would more likely get an MBA or a law degree in two or three years and then work with Wall Street or corporate America. That is not what physicians are about.

Physician's Fees

How typical of the bureaucratic mentality to wish to micromanage every aspect of a physician's practice including the coding of procedures—the means of reimbursement from HMO's and insurance companies. The higher the code, the more the re-imbursement. It is true that Medicare and private insurance companies pay the bills, and he who pays the piper . . . It is also true that some physicians are just plain dishonest. I don't believe it is a majority but it is clearly a presence. A larger number believe that what they are doing merits their coding practice while a significant number believe they are unfairly undercompensated for work they have performed, and they therefore upgrade in order to get what they consider to be a fair fee.

Physicians have made a Faustian bargain with Medicare, HMOs and private insurance companies. They have gained access to large numbers of patients who are insured by one or more of these companies by agreeing to be on the panel and accepting their fee schedule, which is often so low and so difficult to collect in a timely fashion that their cash flow is seriously impaired and many find it difficult to continue in private practice. Faced with such a problem (in government as well as in private industry) bureaucrats respond as bureaucrats are wont to do—with evermore complex rules and regulations, adversarial relations with the physicians, ever more involvement in the physician's practice and ever more complex means of punishment. Exactly the wrong approach.

An alternative approach, based purely on time spent with the patient is also, in my opinion, wrongheaded. A new physician, relatively inexperienced, spends more time with a patient than an older, more experienced physician because the older physician has seen many, many similar patients. Should he be penalized because of his knowledge? Similarly, physician styles differ. Some like to chat with their patients while others go right to their task. Some like to check more things than others do. Some like to give more time to explanations than others do. Making time the dominant factor in coding, and thus in fees, could lead to indifferent medicine where visits are artificially lengthened to qualify for higher fees.

What is the solution? First it should be noted that there is no perfect solution. Every system has its advantages and drawbacks. People—both physicians and patients—differ. Further, in spite of ever more complex rules and regulations, some bad actors will get away with murder. That is unfortunate, but the alternative is the above.

I believe that everything should be made simpler, not more complex, and a relationship should be established with the physicians on the basis of trust, not hostility. After all, the overwhelming majority of physicians are at least as honest as the lay people supervising them, and should be treated that way. By all means go after the bad apples—those who deliberately falsify for financial gain—and punish them severely. They will not get much support from the majority of physicians who are honest and hard working and yet are tarred with the same brush.

How to do that? First, simplify the codes. From the five or six codes which apply to the patient visit, reduce them to three: New Patient, Follow Up, and Brief Follow Up. There should be rare cases of Extended Follow Up (with appropriate documentation). These coding fees should be compared with others of a similar nature supplied by a fellow practitioner in the same specialty (allowing latitude for experience, normal human variation, etc.). I would be less concerned with such variations than with code variations. Someone who is consistently coding high would be visited by someone from the insurance company who would ask for an explanation for the variation in coding. If the explanation offered by the physician is not satisfactory, then he or she should know that if there were not a change in pattern, an extensive and expensive audit would be forthcoming. Bills will not be paid until the audit is completed. Not a perfect solution, of course, but less hostile than the relationship that exists today.

Professional Courtesy

There has been much discussion in the recent past about professional courtesy—physicians treating other

80

physicians and their nuclear families for free—or at least for whatever the insurance companies will pay. The argument made is that physicians can afford it and therefore they should pay for services rendered like anyone else.

First, to me, it is not a burden but a distinct honor to have a fellow physician place himself or his family in my care. To trust me in that fashion, putting their life and health in my hands, says much about my standing in the medical community. Although becoming more and more like a trade, medicine is still a profession, and respect for one's colleagues is manifested by treatment without a fee. The one difficulty I have with this is the treatment of psychiatrists, since they do not offer professional courtesy to other physicians. Indeed I had one psychiatrist who did not live in my community, did not practice medicine in my community, did not refer patients to me, but who insisted on professional courtesy. To top it off, he carried very inexpensive health insurance, since he did not expect to pay physicians their fees. In other words, he was making a profit on our backs. Aside from that individual, I take care of this problem on a case-by-case basis.

A second problem, relatively rare for me but more common for university physicians, was what to do about physicians who referred themselves or their families, but did not live or practice in the community. Here too, when faced with this problem, I handled it on a case by case basis.

The next argument is that if one does not charge the patient, one should not accept the payment from the insurance company. I have difficulty understanding that concept. After all, the patient does pay the premiums. The treating physician does do the work. What his policy is with regard to collection of fees should be his own business. After all, we are talking about a lowering of fees, not a raising of them. The whole issue, to my mind, is a foolish and non-issue issue, since the overwhelming majority of physicians will continue to be honored to serve their colleagues and their families.

Rating of Providers

In a front page article in the *Washington Post* of June 5, 2001 the Health Care Financing Agency (HCFA) announces that it is planning to issue detailed ratings of the quality of care provided, an evaluation which will eventually include all health care providers. The object is to provide consumers and government overseers with an objective numerical rating system upon which care can be evaluated.

There is much to praise about such a system. As they have noted in the article, they can focus on those "bad actors" that provide inferior or unacceptable care and try to bring them up to acceptable levels or shut them down. Consumers can have a guideline when they are seeking care, and one can be sure that most providers will make every effort to improve their ratings, presumably for the benefit of their consumers.

There are definite downsides to the proposal however. The ratings system has to assume that the populations being treated are equal if one is to make a judgment about the quality of care being given. That is definitely not the case since some providers treat far sicker populations than others. Without question it will lead to gaming the system to produce a favorable outcome. Sicker patients will be excluded from care. Subtle changes in diagnostic coding will take place, both on admission and discharge to lessen the responsibility for complications. For example, the admission to a nursing home of a patient with a reddening of the skin and the smallest abrasion will be coded as a decubitus ulcer to offset the possibility that the patient will actually develop a decubitus ulcer while in the nursing home. Discharge diagnoses will likely underplay any complications so that they are not held against the institution. The same will be carried out in physicians' offices. The most important problem, however, is how to deal with an individual or institution that feels that they are being dealt with unfairly. There has to be an appeals process that is both fair and rapid. It does little good to exonerate someone or some institution after such a long time that irreparable harm has been done.

If, however, it has been decided to proceed with ratings, shouldn't the party that everyone detests, the insurance companies, also be rated? I suggested to my medical society that they do just that, but they declined. However, the government might be able to do that and post copies of the annual or semi-annual ratings in every post office or online. On further thought, how about rating the raters? Shouldn't HCFA also be rated? Courtesy, promptness in answering complaints and inquiries, promptness in making payments, lessening of red tape and many other categories could easily be rated, with the results put on the Internet and forwarded to the appropriate Congressional committee which oversees the budget for the agency. When they show a willingness to submit themselves to a system they prescribe for others, I will breathe a sigh of relief and say they should go ahead.

The Float

One would think that the money earned by insurance companies comes directly from the premiums paid by the subscribers. Money taken in minus expenses (overhead plus payments to providers) equals profit. That is, of course, true. A well-run insurance company will have outgo less than income, and hence profit. However, a major source of income comes from the float—moneys taken in but not yet disbursed. The moneys not yet disbursed do not sit in a drawer but are invested for a nice profit. Since we are talking about billions and billions of dollars, we are talking about a very large sum of money indeed. Hence, the insurance companies can do, and will do, anything to delay payment.

Here are just some of the extraordinary lengths to which insurance companies will go in order to delay payment to a provider. The first thing they say is that they did not receive the bill for services rendered. They say that even if the bill was sent electronically so that they must have received it. Then they say that it is filed the wrong way, and since every insurance company has different rules for filing and there are hundreds of insurance companies providing health insurance they could be right—at least technically. After that, they claim it is the wrong code (for the procedure performed by the provider) or it is an incomplete code. Time passes. They then ask the provider to provide a letter of justification. This is then placed under "review." The reviewers may be in-house but more often are outside consultants under contract to the insurance company. How would you guess they find in the vast majority of reviews? You would be right of course, since they, the reviewers, know which side their bread is buttered on.

Another ploy is for the insurance company to say that they do not cover that procedure. After several phone calls and screaming matches they admit that they do, in fact, cover the procedure in question. So sorry. They then complain that the fee is far too high and they will not pay it. One can, of course, appeal but that adds weeks and weeks to the process and during that time the funds are not available to the provider. Finally they agree that payment will be made and the funds are "in the mail." That is a figurative rather than a literal expression since only a certain number of approved payments are actually put in the mail each day.

By and large, providers are small business people with fixed expenses which must be met every month: payroll, rent, utilities, etc. Extra staff must be hired to fight with the insurance companies, adding to the overhead. Since expenses are fixed and must be met, it is sometimes far easier to just accept the payment offered, even if not felt to be fair, than to fight and have no cash flow to meet expenses. Such is the battle against the float.

Victims

It seems as if everyone wants to be a victim. If the categories of victims were reportable to the Center for Disease Control (CDC), they would be unable to function because of overwork. Look at what you get from being a victim. Vast outpourings of sympathy. Special legislation. Gobs of publicity. The excitement of organizing, picketing, marching. Financial benefits. The list goes on. It started with race. Soon added were gender, ethnic origin, and sexual orientation. Now we are into biologic characteristics. It used to be that people who were short, obese, homely or born with a physical handicap chalked it up to bad genes or bad luck. Now they are victims, and society must pay them, one way or the other, for their victimization. Even growing old is a form of victimization.

Along with the ever-growing lists of victims, has grown the use of euphemisms. People now are vertically disadvantaged, physically challenged or the victim of "ageism." A recent medical article described prostitutes as commercial sex workers. Now really! These euphemisms are really a form of magic. If you don't say the words, then the condition doesn't exist. Soon this will spread to medical diseases where people will be neoplastically challenged or endocrinologically disadvantaged.

Because of the above, I believe physicians should become victims. In addition to all of the above mentioned benefits, patients will take pity. As a result some patients will pay their bills on time. Others will return money that they collected from insurance companies to pay medical bills. Still others will make a conscious effort to hold down on the paperwork they inflict on their doctor. Pete Stark, Ralph Nader, Sidney Wolfe and countless editorialists will have nice words to say about us. The possibilities seem endless. But of what are we to be the victims? We could say stress brought about by years of sacrifice and hard work. Better than that, we can claim to be victims of success. All the retirees sitting around the nineteenth hole or their condo pool and complaining about the high cost of medicine forget that one or two generations ago people of their age had a more peaceful existence. Those on the golf course with total hips or knees, on the tennis courts with coronary artery grafts, leading a productive life with organ replacement, kidney failure or paraplegia also seem to forget. So man the barricades! Hoist the placards! Let's become victims too.

(*Virginia Medical Quarterly*, Summer 1994)

86

Women and Medicine

The title of this essay refers to the treatment of women as patients and the treatment of women as physicians. This is an issue of great moment now with claims made of gross mistreatment and gross under-treatment of women. As in all important issues, there is some element of truth in these claims, but unfortunately, there is a great deal of falseness as well. I have no doubt that there are (and were, with more in the past than in the present) male physicians who were chauvinists who treated women with less than full respect and tended to underplay some women's problems. On the other side, there are some women who have axes to grind and causes to follow, are less than fully concerned about the truth and who in turn are blinded by dislike of men. There is certainly a lot of stereotypical thinking going on.

First, women as patients. I have never seen a serious medical problem, nor have I heard about such, treated as anything other than a serious medical problem, no matter what the gender of the patient. The problem arises when the condition is less than life threatening, particularly when nothing specific can be found to explain the symptoms. A somewhat cavalier attitude then arises, and women are right when they detect, either by verbal or non-verbal signs, such an attitude. It is certainly not universal, but it is present, and male physicians have to be aware of it.

A second claim is made that woman patients are not treated fairly in clinical testing. They claim that they are underutilized in clinical testing and that less money and fewer clinical trials are directed towards women's problems. The under-utilization in clinical trials largely refers to the use of women in cardiac disease trials, particularly coronary artery disease trials. It has to be understood that this has nothing to do with prejudice but to an historic truth—cardiac disease was largely a male disease until very recently. With extended life expectancy, women are now lucky enough to live long enough to start getting heart disease, and so they should be included in clinical trials. And of course they will be.

The dollars expended, and number of clinical trials, for women's diseases, is loudly claimed to be too little as compared to men. My reading of the information available from the National Institutes of Health is that this is simply not true; in fact, it is the opposite of truth. There are more clinical trials and more dollars spent on women's diseases such as breast cancer and uterine and ovarian cancer than is present for male diseases such as prostate cancer. But what does the truth have to do with anything when there is a cause to be fought?

Second, women in medicine. There has been such a dramatic change in the admission of women into medical school that it is difficult for me to comprehend. When I was in medical school there were no more than five or six females in a class of one hundred and fifty. Now there is close to parity and I have been told that there will soon be a majority of women in medical school and hence in medicine. One may believe this is good or it is bad, but it is a fact. It is also a fact that the world changes, but not necessarily smoothly or painlessly.

I have observed that there are differences between male and female physicians. These are not necessarily good or bad; they are just there. First, females and males are able to absorb the enormous amount of information that goes into the making of a physician equally; perhaps females even have an edge. Second, females are better able to relate to the whole patient rather than the affected organ or organ system. They seem to have more empathy for the patient as a whole than do males. There seems to be little difference in the quality of the care given by males and females, but males appear to be more aggressive, more driven and more entrepreneurial, thus creating new means and new techniques of providing care. They are also more willing to take risks. These characteristics, of course, are generalizations, but in the main I believe they are true. Further, females have other, biologic, demands on them, namely the bearing and rearing of children which require a great deal of time and energy. Thus, females are more willing to work part time or in salaried positions so that they have time for child rearing.

A final problem brought up by females is their role in academia. I have never been in academia so cannot comment first hand but I have heard much discussion about the subject. There are clearly fewer women in academia, in the top echelons of the academic hierarchy and in research. I suspect that there is no one reason for this, but rather a compilation of factors. Some undoubtedly is due to prejudice by males, particularly in the surgical specialties, in some to the demands of the biologic clock, and some due to the innate aggressiveness of males as they claw their way up the academic ladder. I cannot ascribe percentages to any one factor, but I suspect it varies from case to case.

I believe there is some element of fairness in the claims of women as being victims as patients as well as being physicians. It is, however, markedly overdone and further is clearly changing, as is obvious to anyone who has had a lengthy longitudinal view of medicine. This will not deter those women who have a stake in being victims, and reaping the benefits of such a state.

Private Practice Issues

Compulsory Medical Education

To enter the profession of medicine is to embark upon a lifetime commitment to education. In that sense, continuing medical education (CME) is simply an expression of that commitment. In twenty-two states, continuing medical education credits are now required for licensure (Virginia is not among them); many medical societies require CME credits for membership (including the Medical Society of Virginia); and most specialty boards require CME credits for recertification.

We are beginning to see the undesirable side effects of mandatory continuing medical education. By this time we all passively accept the increased record keeping, the outrageously high cost of acquiring the appropriate credits, the hypocrisy involved in taking a cruise or vacationing on a tropical isle while taking a course for CME credit. I personally have lost the embarrassment of asking whether I will be getting CME credit for a course, lecture, or seminar, rather than just wondering whether it will be interesting or beneficial to me. It seems the dim past, although it is only a few years ago, when we physicians could choose on our own what was necessary to further our education.

Compulsory CME is simply not the best way to further a physician's growth in knowledge and ability. It uses only the negative connotation of punishment, rather than any true positive reward. Yet we have seen a whole new industry developed for providing, documenting, and judging of CME, all this at a high cost to be paid for in state and national society dues, in the cost of the meetings, and in the extra work and documentation in our offices. Of course this expense is passed on to our patients. Although there is evidence that knowledge is gained from CME (this of course has always been true), there is no evidence that it significantly alters practice. Without ever more complex and onerous controls, how does one deal with someone who arrives late at a meeting or leaves early, who daydreams through the program, or who takes a brief catnap, particularly in postprandial or evening meetings? How do we prove that what was presented was learned? How do we prove that what was learned was applied? How do we prove that what was applied alters the outcomes? I am not arguing against altered (improved) outcomes, nor the fact that increased knowledge is a factor (but not the only factor) in improved outcomes—only the means of proving it via forced education.

There is an implied assumption, based on the methods of our schooldays, that most learning comes from a formal setting wherein a teacher passes on knowledge to a student who supplements the classroom knowledge with "homework." Although I am sure that this continues to hold true to some extent throughout the clinical years, I doubt that this makes up the bulk of applied knowledge. Methods of learning are highly individualized. Some learn best in solitude, others in a crowd. Some need background noise (music or voices), some need complete quiet. Some learn best by visual means (watching a tape, reading a book, or direct observation), some by oral means (discussions, seminars), some by aural means (lectures, cassette tapes, CDs), and most by a combination of these. It is my strong suspicion that far more applied clinical knowledge is learned in hospital corridors and nursing stations, doctors' lounges, hospital cafeterias and in telephone discussions with other physicians of patient problems than by any formal CME program. (This is probably not true of basic knowledge, which must be transmitted in a more formal setting.)

One view expressed early on was that if we did not do something about policing our profession, the government would. Well, we have done something and Congress, in the person of Representative Fortney "Pete" Stark, has responded in a predictable fashion. He has introduced HR 4464, which, if passed (not likely for now, but a portent for the future), would mandate that physicians would have to take a proficiency examination if they are to be permitted to treat Medicare patients (*American Medical News*, 4 May 1990). So much for the theory that lawmakers could be held off if we embarked on self-policing. Our professional organizations ought to insist that if repeated testing is the measure of proficiency, then Congress ought to lead the way. Not only members of Congress but their legislative assistants ought to be required to be examined periodically on U.S. history, the U.S. Constitution, and constitutional law, political science, economics, and, most importantly, ethics. Those who fail the testing should be forced to give up their positions and leave Washington so they cannot end up with lucrative "consulting" positions, all too often a euphemism for influence peddling.

We of course have an obligation to protect the welfare of the patient under treatment while at the same time being scrupulously fair to the physician. In the hospital this can be accomplished by credentialing the physician not only for general admitting privileges in his or her specialty but also for the performance of specific procedures. Under an agreed upon process, the removal of the right to do these procedures can be revoked for cause. In the physician's office, a periodic chart review process should be instituted whereby outside physicians come in and randomly review some charts. This is a process which should be paid for by the physician under review, which will be seen as worthwhile if a frank discussion is held at the end of the review and the good and bad features of the observed treatment is discussed. More learning would take place from that than from attending many conferences—far less expensive as well, since no income is earned when the physician is away from the office attending a course. Of course, people will learn to treat charts, but wise reviewers would see through that.

There is another proposal I would make. On the 10th anniversary of graduation from medical school and every ten years thereafter, I propose a compulsory return to school (preferably one's own medical school) of approximately three weeks. Although beneficial from an education standpoint (for example, the first week could be devoted to basic science, the second to general clinical medical advances, and the third to advances in one's own and related specialties), the basic purpose would be renewal for the physician. This would be both physical and mental renewal. Activities outside the formal classroom environment would include basic health parameters performed on each physician, with follow-ups to see that corrective measures are taken; organized discussions of subjects ranging from medical ethics to the management of impaired physicians to practice problems to health policy matters; and of course renewing old acquaintances in a relaxed and informal environment. This could give each physician the psychic energy to face the coming decade (*Virginia Medical Quarterly*, Autumn 1990).

Dear Provider

More and more frequently now I receive mail with the request (demand) for additional information or explanation (justification) of treatment addressed by the salutation "Dear Provider." No name. No hard-earned title. Just "Dear Provider." Right up there with the purveyors of trusses and support stockings. How dare we think we are entitled to some elementary courtesy? These letter writers certainly know how to put us in our place.

The letter, however, always contains a signature (they at least are real people), often followed by a string of letters, abbreviations for unknown titles. It seems that the number of letters following the name are inversely proportional to people's knowledge of their meaning. How to answer such letters, as well as other annoying "requests," has troubled me. Two examples for each salutation are given, depending on their snideness and on your mood. Feel free to make up your own.

Insurance Company
Polite—Dear Payer
Less polite—Dear Gouger

Rehabilitation Nurse
Polite—Dear Intermediary
Less polite—Dear Meddler

Government Agency
Polite—Dear Public Functionary
Less polite—Dear Bureaucrat

Claims Adjustors
Polite—Dear Doubter
Less polite—Dear Know It All

Independent Reviewer (Challenging the Treatment)
Polite—Dear Expert
Less polite—Dear So-called Expert

Patients with Multiple Forms to Fill Out
Polite—Dear Trying My Patience
Less polite—Dear Pest

Lawyer
Polite—Dear Contingent Worker
Less polite—Dear (Fill in the Blank)

Not much perhaps but just one more indignity visited upon us as we try as best we can to go about our business.
(*Virginia Medical Quarterly*, Winter 1995)

Early Physician Retirement

There is scarcely a self-employed physician over the age of fifty who is not only planning to retire but actually taking steps toward that goal. This is a completely new phenomenon since in the past physicians typically died in harness. For others, they continued to practice until they became so old and feeble that their patients left them for younger physicians, forcing them into involuntary retirement. Many died shortly thereafter. In addition to the above, an interesting side issue has developed—the issue of retirement on disability. Previously, providing disability insurance for physicians was very lucrative for the insurance companies since physicians persisted in their work even with existing pain and disability. Now physicians want out and many of them are eligible for disability insurance. To say the least, insurance companies are not happy campers.

I don't believe society recognizes the seriousness of the loss of a whole generation of senior physicians. Leaving aside the really elderly physicians who probably should be required to retire, physicians between the ages of fifty and seventy have an enormous gift to offer society. Although younger physicians probably know more in terms of theory and new developments in medicine (not an insignificant point by any means), older physicians have a huge amount of clinical experience. It is one thing to know something in theory and another to know about it from multiple repetitions. Some patients like to think their problem is completely unique ("Have you seen this before, doctor?"). It may be true for a few rare cases, but most are simply a repetition of what has been seen before.

The practice of medicine involves mistakes. You don't want to hear about it? I can't blame you. These mistakes may be of commission but more likely of omission. Learning from experience and from mistakes produces wisdom. Wisdom helps to know when to act and when to observe. When to order tests and when not. When to know what the patient's wishes are, whether expressed verbally or not.

By and large, physicians over fifty have paid off their student loans, sent their children through college (and graduate school), bought a house with most of it paid off, and practice medicine for the sheer pleasure of it. They of course expect to be compensated for their services but pleasure in their work is the dominant theme. The loss of a significant portion of senior physicians (and, incidentally, other health professionals as well) is not good for America's health.

The Importance of Touching

"He never even examined me!" How often I have heard that from a patient? On further questioning it is almost always untrue. What the patient really meant was that the physician never touched him/her except through the intervention of a piece of equipment such as a stethoscope or a reflex hammer. It is ironic that as we have added decades to life expectancy, essentially erased childhood infectious diseases and added enormously to the survival and well-being of our patients, they have appreciated us less and less. The reasons for this are manifold, but I do believe one factor is that we have transformed ourselves into the providers of technology rather than performing our traditional role as healers.

When we had limited resources for diagnosis (and treatment) available to us, a meticulous physical examination was essential. That of course meant touching the patient. Now the technology is so superior that it appears to become far more important than what we can find through fingers, ears and brains. Therefore a very superficial examination preceding the ordering or performing of a battery of expensive testing makes the physician seem to be impersonal and uncaring. A patient related to me the story that she was referred to a world famous endoscopist for a colonoscopy. Having never met the doctor, she was lying in the lateral decubitus position (on her side) in preparation for her study when she saw him enter in scrub suit and mask. She said to him "Doctor, would you mind if I saw your face?" Whereupon he lowered his mask, smiled, replaced it and proceeded to the colonoscopy without ever having said a word. An extreme example, of course, but clearly demonstrating the doctor as super-technician and not physician/healer. Most medical schools and residency programs appear to concentrate on turning out as an end product doctors, by which I mean scientist/technologist, and spend very little time in teaching them to be physicians, by which I mean confidants and healers. Not for a moment do I suggest that objectivity and the ability to make difficult decisions under trying circumstances be lost, but there is surely more to medicine than ordering tests and performing procedures.

Most of the non-medical specialists with whom I come in contact: nurses, physical and occupational therapists, myotherapists, chiropractors as well as osteopathic physicians who still do manipulation all do extensive "laying on of hands" in the course of their work. I believe this is one of the factors which spares them from the hostility reserved for physicians, although of course this is not the only factor. In the course of a hospitalization of a patient, the least important thing for a physician to do on a particular day might be to examine the patient. Obtaining lab results, talking to the radiologist, the pathologist, the physical therapist, etc., arranging for a consultation, discovering the patient's behavior and response to treatment with the nurses may all take precedence over the examining of the patient. Yet to the patient, the all-important event of the day is the physician's visit and in particular the physician's hands checking the pulse, examining the abdomen, etc. It takes very little time and effort and yet may bring a gratifying response from the patient ("He really cares!"). Further, a great deal of trouble can be avoided by contriving to examine the patient when the real purpose of the visit was to explain something to the patient. The same is particularly true in an office setting. It doesn't happen often but frequently enough to raise my blood pressure that an extraordinary amount of energy is expended trying to explain with words, diagrams, models, etc. a procedure or test which is to be undergone or to explain the nature of the illness. The patient then complains bitterly when the bill is received: "I don't know why I was charged—he did nothing but talk to me." A simple, even cursory examination may help to prevent that problem.

A great deal of my practice involved soft tissue injuries. Many of these problems can be detected only with the principal diagnostic tool being the examining fingers—still a potent weapon when used carefully. It is not often understood that these problems are not trivial but may cause severe pain and disability, even if they are not life threatening. A recognition of these two facts—that these problems can only be detected by manual examination and that the pain caused may be very severe—has permitted me to help solve some perplexing problems. For example, a patient came to me reporting that she had severe pain in the upper back which radiated through to her thorax. She was initially hospitalized by a cardiologist who did a complete cardiac and pulmonary work-up and concluded that there was nothing wrong with her thoracic viscera and sent her home. The pain persisted and the patient sought out a neurologist who did a thorough investigation of her spinal neuraxis as well as her upper GI tract and found nothing. He too discharged her whereupon she was referred to me. Her story again emphasized that the pain originated in the upper back and from there to the thorax and anterior chest. On palpation of the back, there was exquisite tenderness in the musculature which immediately reproduced her pain (a sure sign of the little-known but ubiquitous myofascial pain). Local injection brought about significant reduction in pain and a brief further course of injections and therapy brought about its cessation. The comment of the patient was instructive. She stated that she told each of the consulting physicians where her pain was but none of them touched her—they only ordered additional tests. Here was a very practical—not just psychological—reason for touching the patient, and one that is not uncommon.

We have serious problems in medicine today and touching the patient is not going to cure them. However it is an obvious way that we have to demonstrate our concern for their problems, to bond ourselves to them and to show that we are healers in the long tradition of medicine and not simply the appliers of modern technology and the dispensers of magical pills. Try it.

(*Virginia Medical Quarterly*, Summer 1993)

It's So Expensive

It is often stated, and indeed was the thesis behind the ill-fated Clinton health plan and the eventual rise of Health Maintenance Organizations (HMOs), that medical care was "too expensive." Nobody can doubt the rising cost of health care and its consumption of a larger and ever-growing percentage of the nation's GDP expenditures. However, nobody can say for certain what exactly is the appropriate expenditure for health care in this wealthiest of all nations. It is true that most of the nation's hospitals were run with less than optimal business efficiency, but at the time they didn't see themselves as profit driven entities; but as public service entities—and heavily labor intensive ones at that. Most of the gross inefficiencies have been wrung out of hospitals, as they have out of physician offices, but the cost of medical care continues to rise.

Much of the ire against the high expenses of medical care was directed against the physicians, whose direct costs to the public, in actuality, make up less than 20 percent of the health care dollar. What is not appreciated is that while it is true that physicians hospitalize patients and order tests and treatments, they get paid only for their professional services. They therefore do not benefit financially from the ordering of tests and treatment. In their offices, physicians are faced with enormous overheads—usually 50–60 percent of gross income (and gross income is significantly below gross billings), a side of the equation that patients do not see when they get a copy of their bill. This is in part due to painfully high liability insurance as well as extra staffing needed to fight the battles for reimbursement with the insurance companies. One can complain that too many tests are being done by physicians, a judgment which may or may not be true, but every day a physician faces this dilemma—order a test which he suspects will be negative, or not order it, eventually find in rare cases that it was positive, and then face a lawsuit. A new entry in the equation is the HMO which dictates, by a mechanistic approach, not having any knowledge of the specific patient, what tests can be ordered and what treatment can be rendered. By contrast, patients just want their problem solved. How often have I heard, "Don't worry about the cost, doc, I have insurance."

My experience has been that there are basically three categories of patients. The first is the worried well. A few among these patients want objective confirmation in the form of tests, tests and more tests, but most seek reassurance that they do not have anything seriously wrong and are satisfied if so reassured. The second category of patient has minor or self-limited problems that require proper diagnosis and treatment, but they pose no threat to life and are often likely to be cured with the simple passage of time. These first two categories of patients will question proposed diagnostic and treatment measures, particularly if it involves out-of-pocket costs. The third category is those patients in which it seems clear that something serious is happening. Those patients want nothing but the best treatment available, and hang the expense. They seldom question the treatment plan except in terms of choices.

The odd thing about medical care is that most people are well most of the time. They—the well—make decisions about the ill, or I should say about other's illnesses, for all too often they act in an appropriate fashion when they or theirs are facing a serious medical problem.

Therefore, when people say, "It's too expensive," one can be reasonably sure that they are basically healthy and their involvement with medical care is primarily the payment of the monthly premiums. When it is their turn (and it comes to all of us) to be seriously ill, cost is miraculously factored out and their only concern is getting well. That of course is natural, but it does have more than a slight trace of irony.

Layering of Care

Historically, the care provided patients could roughly be divided into three layers. The affluent could afford the best care available: the best doctors, the best hospitals, the best services, etc. The indigent were cared for at the municipal hospitals or on the charity wards of private hospitals where they served as teaching cases for the house staff, while the middle class fended for itself—it paid when it could, negotiated when it could not and went to the charity wards when necessary. The advent of health insurance for essentially all working people after WWII changed all of that. Excluding items of personal comfort such as a private room, specially prepared food, etc. everyone with insurance was treated virtually the same. The same doctors provided the same diagnostic and therapeutic procedures at the same hospitals as was provided to the very affluent. The indigent were still treated in the same fashion as before, but if an individual worked and had health insurance he received the same care as others regardless of social status. This has all changed with the advent of new forms of health insurance.

Care is now layered in a different way. If the patient is on a capitation plan, or even in an HMO (Health Maintenance Organization), the object is to have the physician see the patient as little as possible. Since physicians are the highest paid on the provider food chain (not as high as administrators of course), the HMO wishes to minimize their use so that additional physicians will not have to be provided. Patients, of course, are taken care of, but the initial work, and much of the follow up work is provided by nurses, nurse practitioners, physician assistants, etc. In a capitation system, the physician or physician group is paid a fixed annual fee to provide complete medical care for that patient. If the patient consumes more care than is provided by the capitation amount allotted, the physician must cover that cost overrun personally, by writing a check to the insurance company. Therefore he may actually lose money if forced to see the patient in the office, hospitalize the patient, etc. What a sad state of affairs and what a dreadful dilemma for the physician.

If the physician still sees patients on a fee-for-service basis, the insurance companies provide less and less reimbursement accompanied by more and more hassle. This is accompanied by stable, or even rising, expenses. The physician is therefore obligated to see more and more patients, either lengthening the working day or crowding more patients into the schedule. This cannot help but lower the quality of care provided each patient. The changes may be subtle but they are clearly there. We now have a different method of layering of care, but I am not sure it is any better than the old method.

My Medical Care Transition

I have been a witness to an extraordinary journey in medicine covering seven decades. In the nineteen thirties and forties, I was far too young to be in medicine, but my father was in medicine. His training in the nineteen twenties wasn't far different from that at the turn of the century—the beginning of the age of modern medicine, of anesthesia, x-rays, EKG's, the concepts of sterilization, invasive surgery, the rudiments of laboratory medicine, etc.

The Early Years: Medicine in the Thirties, Forties and Fifties was extraordinarily primitive by today's standards. My father, like most of his compatriots, practiced medicine out of his house. That really put a strain on family life since noise was verboten and dinner was timed religiously to be between afternoon and evening office hours. The striking thing to me about medical care then was the extraordinary number of hours put in by physicians. Specialists, such as my father, had a somewhat more regulated life but GPs (General Practitioners), whom I had a chance to observe closely, were essentially on call twenty-four hours per day, seven days a week. The only break was to sign out to someone else for a brief period of time. Group practices were unknown. In rare instances, OB/GYN physicians would have a group of two or three.

House calls were common and appropriate. After all, there was little more that a physician could do in his office than what he could carry in his black satchel. It was a very inefficient way of seeing patients, but most physicians were struggling to keep their patients and make a living. The making of a living was extremely difficult for most physicians. My father told me that it was common practice for patients with nighttime emergencies to call several physicians and the first one to get there saw the patient. The others were just out of luck. Also, the fees were usually paid in cash and what the government didn't know didn't hurt them. It should be noted that house calls are still appropriate for people such as the frail elderly with a chronic problem in order to see what is going on more than to provide definitive treatment, and are done by conscientious physicians.

Most physicians would spend their mornings on house calls or make rounds at the hospital and then have afternoon and evening office hours. Many of the physicians—in spite of long hours and low pay—donated significant amounts of time staffing charity clinics at the various hospitals until such practice fell out of favor, because giving "charity" was looked down upon. Another link in the chain of serving as a duty of physicians broken.

The practice of medicine in the office of that day was primitive compared to today's office medicine. Some physicians had an x-ray machine (I shudder to think of the amount of radiation escaping from those primitive and poorly monitored machines), an EKG machine and were able to do a CBC (Complete Blood Count) and urinalysis, and little more. Diagnosis was by history and physical examination—far better than what is done today—but certainly not sensitive to early findings since the physical findings needed to be far more advanced before they were found on physical examination. By the same token, hospitals were not much better. Of course they could do somewhat more extensive laboratory studies and radiographically they relied on plain x-rays and tomography (plain x-rays done in body slices). For studying the spine, myelography (injecting dye into the spine and then taking x-rays) was done. For studying the brain pneumoencephalography (injecting air into the ventricles of the brain and then taking x-rays), plus a few others such as EEGs (electroencephalograms) were the range of diagnostic testing. Hospitals in that era did not have anesthesia induction rooms, recovery rooms, cardiac care units, medical intensive care units, surgical intensive care units and many other features of a modern hospital. The nurses, too, were generalists, taking care of medical and surgical patients as they came. Of course major surgery could be performed but an incredibly long convalescence was thought to be necessary, which led to such serious complications as pulmonary embolus (a clot of blood which escaped from the leg and migrated to the lung). The same held true for treatment of myocardial infarction secondary to coronary artery thrombosis. The standard treatment was three weeks in bed without moving a muscle. During my medical school days, a huge crowd consisting of professors, residents, interns, lowly medical students and nurses watched with intense interest as the chair program of Dr. Samuel Lavine of Boston was instituted. The patient was gotten up from bed and seated in a chair after only two weeks of bed rest. This was considered revolutionary.

Having made the diagnosis, treatment was instituted. If surgery was performed, it was for the most part done by skilled surgeons, although it was not unusual for GPs to do major abdominal surgery or for general surgeons to do orthopedic or gynecologic or urologic surgery. As late as the late fifties, I saw one procedure (a mastectomy) being done by an internist, to the obvious disgust of the surgeons. The surgeries, although often skillfully done, were relatively crude and invasive in a major way so that recuperation was long and slow. The era was characterized by a remarkably small pharmacopeia. If lucky there were one or two drugs available for each major medical condition. By the end of internship, or certainly residency, one knew the entire formulary—even if not using the drugs oneself. Think of an era when there were no antibiotics, no steroids (cortisone), no medicines for hypertension, only insulin for diabetes, digitalis for heart failure and virtually no drugs for serious neurologic disorders—Parksinsonism, cerebral palsy, congenital neurological problems, etc. Even when I was in medical school, the most meticulous neurological examination leading to a diagnosis was demonstrated but after the diagnosis was made, essentially no treatment was available. Not only were there no treatments for lipid disorders, they were essentially terra incognita. Even when I was in medical school in the fifties a year's course of Biochemistry devoted just two weeks to the study of lipid disorders, and that was of the most general thoughts. It has to be noted that physicians and hospital personnel were devoted but simply did not have the tools for modern medical care.

The Middle Years: I consider the years from my entrance to medical school in the early fifties to the late seventies and early eighties to be my middle years in medical care transition. Looking back, these were very exciting and fulfilling years, but they also set the stage for the troubles that exist today. World War II brought about a huge jump in medical knowledge and in the provision of medical care. After the war and starting from virtually nothing, every major suburb of a city developed its own health system, including major new hospitals, clinics, medical office buildings with specialists, pharmacies, etc. Before this, the pattern was GPs in the suburbs, who referred their more difficult cases to specialists and hospitals in the city—quite a change since gradually the suburban hospitals grew in diversity of services and of quality, the better ones eventually matching the best of the city hospitals. Ironically, towards the end of this period the city hospitals staggering under the burden of care to huge indigent populations, began a decline that continues to this day.

Research proliferated and a stream of new diagnostic and treatment tools emerged. It started with the sulfa drugs and penicillin, and shortly thereafter with corticosteroids (cortisone) but spread rapidly in all directions.

New surgical procedures appeared with dazzling speed. I remember being allowed, as a medical student, to stand in the back of the operating room and watch the first mitral valvulotomy being performed at the hospital. It was being done to free up the valves of the heart which had become frozen together (so that they could not function well) due to the ravages of rheumatic fever. Yes, rheumatic fever secondary to infection from the streptococcus bacteria was still commonplace. There was also a contagion ward at the city hospital where I trained, with row after row of kids with diphtheria, mumps, measles (all with complications) because vaccines were not yet common.

To perform the surgical procedure I was watching, the surgeon needed to actually enter the upper heart chamber (the atrium) of the beating heart and with a finger or small myotome (knife) separate the valves. The tension in the room was palpable. Yet in only a few years this was considered to be a procedure of such simplicity that it was given to the resident to perform. It is now primarily of historic interest since rheumatic fever has largely ceased to exist. All other fields of medicine showed similar growth. As knowledge, training and ability grew, specialties and subspecialties proliferated. This was not primarily because of increased income for specialists, although surely that was a factor, but rather because of the rapid growth of knowledge which required full time attention to smaller and smaller areas of medicine.

Increased training and increased knowledge are, and should be, rewarded. The larger idea that the majority of people who became physicians because of income is ludicrous. If income were primary, why spend all those extra years in labs while in college, as well as eight to ten years after college graduation in medical school, internship, residency and fellowship, all for money. Better to get an MBA in two years and then work for a corporation, for a business or on Wall Street. Why give up a whole decade or more of one's young life in exciting, but terribly difficult and demanding and impoverished years, just to make money. Rather, most physicians (I agree that not all) want to serve in a noble profession which helps mankind, which is intellectually stimulating and which provides both status and respect. At least that was the way it was in my middle years.

Although often denigrated as simply overly specialized (a small—very small—case can be made for that), the real driving force behind specialization was the explosion of knowledge. It was simply impossible for a generalist to keep up with the new advances in diagnosis and treatment. Thus both medicine and surgery, as well as all other fields of medicine, started specializing and then sub-specializing, each with its own training requirements, boards, etc. Another important factor was the volume of patients seen with a particular problem, and the experience gained from that. One can be reasonably certain that those who criticize specializations the most will run to just such an individual at the first sign of anything considered to be potentially serious. In actuality, it would be a perfectly rational approach.

Another dramatic change came with the advent of medical insurance. It is difficult to believe that there was a time when people did not have health insurance, but there was such a time in nearly half of the twentieth century. What did people do? The best they could. When illness struck they would engage in barter, attempt to have the physician reduce his fees, gather money from

111

the family to pay the fees, or enter the municipal hospital and clinics.

A very small Blue Shield plan for insurance against surgical fees was started in Texas during the late thirties. During World War II, companies could not raise salaries so they threw in health insurance as a benefit. After the war, this benefit spread so that the vast majority of individuals working for large corporations (and later for small businesses as well) were covered against illness by health insurance, which came to be considered a right. Of course, in the early days of insurance medical care was relatively primitive and relatively inexpensive, so it did not pose any great problem to the system. That started to change with the onset of Medicare. Elderly at that time meant people in their sixties, and there were relatively few of them, since so many died off only a few years after retirement. Physicians and their organizations opposed Medicare on the grounds that it would grow uncontrollably. In that aspect they were right. The example of kidney dialysis clearly demonstrated this. Thrown into Medicare for a few tens of million dollars, it has now grown to be in excess of twenty billion dollars per year, and still growing. With tremendous irony, however, what physicians opposed turned out to be a terrific boon for them. Previously, elderly patients were treated by physicians for free, or for greatly discounted fees. This was no longer necessary. And Medicare paid well, at least in the beginning. And they relied on the physician's integrity and judgment (justified in most cases) in the payment of fees. As the number of elderly patients grew, as did the number of diagnostic and treatment measures, the stature, and income, of physicians rose. The same was true with the remainder of the population covered by insurance at the workplace. As shall be shown, however, seeds of problems to come were planted.

Another major problem that reared its head during this period was professional liability. The scourge of lawsuits, virtually unknown in earlier days, had apparently begun to rear its ugly head—however tentatively—in the late fifties when, as a resident, I was told we all had to have liability insurance. Up until then I had never heard of a lawsuit against a physician. So for thirty-five dollars a year I was insured. The process started and has never abated, changing the practice of medicine completely, as will be detailed in the next section.

And what of the physicians themselves? They were still largely the masters of their own fate. Offices had moved from homes to medical arts buildings, complete with pharmacies, x-ray facilities and laboratories as well as other support facilities. All became busy as soon as they hung out a shingle. Groups started to form for hospital and office coverage, for spreading of experiences and for companionship. Although almost all were single specialty groups, there was a start of the multi-specialty group, some of which grew into large clinics serving a wide regional area rather than just the local area. New diagnostic tests and new treatment procedures grew with remarkable rapidity. What would have appeared to be science fiction soon became fact: imaging the inner reaches of the body in a non-invasive fashion; replacement of joints and even organs; replacements of corneas; minimally invasive (endoscopic) surgery; an incredible flow of new drugs and new treatment measures. And with all of this, physicians were able to keep autonomy and to determine what, in their best clinical judgment, was the best course for that particular patient. To experiment, innovate, create new ways of delivering care, to readily take up new procedures—all of these were considered to

113

be in the physicians' domain. Problems with hospital governance were only beginning to appear. In times past the physicians, through their board of directors and committees, ran the hospitals. The administrators did their bidding and the lay board raised the necessary funds. Toward the latter part of the middle years, as the hospitals became much larger, more complex, more specialized and more expensive, administrative ability had to rise, as did administrative authority. And lay boards were no longer content to simply defer to physicians and cover the expenses. They wanted, and were granted, increased authority to make health, and medical, decisions.

Also towards the end of my middle years, the problem of liability started in earnest. At the beginning of my career, topics of discussion by groups of physicians centered about interesting cases, hospital politics and personal matters. Liability gradually became the predominant and ultimately the only topic discussed. A break in the trust between physician and patient started and slowly widened. Testing, as much a means of covering oneself in case of a lawsuit as of obtaining vital information, became the norm. Documenting everything, particularly things that might be questioned later, such as judgment calls, became essential. Physicians started to regard patients not as people in need of help but as potential plaintiffs. What was necessary for the patient and what was necessary for the chart were often different.

For most of this period, physicians were highly regarded and had high status. Towards the end of this period this started to change radically. There is no doubt that physicians were partly to blame. All too many had become aloof and arrogant. Some overcharged and milked the system mercilessly. As specialization proceeded with its undoubted benefits, the relationship between physician and patient deteriorated. It is difficult to have a close relationship when the physician lives in one area, practices in another and the patient comes from a third area. It is difficult to have a close relationship with a sick bone, or organ, or organ system rather than a whole patient. Further, a revolt against authority in general was starting, with people demanding autonomy in determining their care while still holding the physician responsible in case of adverse effects. Some of this was quite rational of course and it came in direct conflict with the paternalistic attitude developed by some physicians, particularly surgeons. Couple that with the overhanging threat of lawsuits and a start towards diminishing physician autonomy in offices and hospitals, and the seeds of trouble for the future were planted. In spite of all this, physicians still devoted enormous amounts of uncompensated time to covering clinics, working on hospital and specialty committees, medical society business, etc.

Recent: The third phase of medical transition started for me in the early eighties and extends to the present time, although I have been retired for the past several years. The earlier devil—continued fear of a liability lawsuit—gave way to the more current, and if possible, greater fear of HMOs and insurance companies, and their effect on medical practice. In earlier times, insurance companies paid reasonably well and reasonably on time. They of course checked carefully on fees that seemed out of line with the usual and customary standards of the community. They also checked carefully on those individuals who seemed to be abusing the system by over-ordering tests or treatments, but otherwise they did not try to micromanage every decision and every fee that the physician made. Therefore it was easy for the physician to accept the patient's insurance, knowing that they would be paid for services rendered in due course. Not fully perhaps, but close enough. How different it is today. Here are some of the things happening today. When no payment is received, the insurance company is called and it claims it never received the bill, even if sent electronically. They claim that the wrong diagnosis or the wrong code is used. They claim that the treatment was unnecessary and they want documentation. They then send it for review to an "independent medical examiner" hired and paid by the insurance company and often in a different specialty or a different part of the same specialty. When the predictable result comes out that the treatment was unnecessary, bargaining begins, with the insurance companies finally agreeing to pay, but only a small fraction of the bill. There is little the physician can do—after all he has ongoing expenses and he is extremely busy with his practice—so he acquiesces. This is not just a few isolated cases but the usual method of operation of the insurance companies. They also practice prevention by requiring pre-approval of any significant treatment measure, including hospitalization. The physician then must make his case for the proposed treatment over the phone to a nurse, or more commonly a clerk. Just think about it: A highly trained and skilled professional who knows the patient and what is best for him/her, must beg (or shout at) a clerk or nurse who has far less training, and who does not know the patient at all. If permission is granted it is often provisional—i.e. only part of the treatment can be used, drug choices are limited, hospital stay limited, etc.

The same situation holds true for the HMOs. They (for the most part) came into being in the wake of the disastrous Clinton health proposal of 1993. Their raison d'être was to save money. Early on they were able to do this as economics of size were brought to bear. This was regarded so highly initially that it was felt to be the wave of the future. This was reflected in the publicly traded companies in their stock prices. With time, however, and after the initial economic savings were made, the process of saving still more money to generate more profits seemed to stall. At this point they honed in on expenses. The physicians and their patients were seen as little more than an expense item on their balance sheet. These expenses were kept under control by denying care, limiting care and denying or limiting payment to health providers. To protect themselves, physicians joined in ever-larger groups so that they could negotiate more like equals. The flaw in that strategy was that to the large hospital groups, HMOs and insurance companies, one physician or physician group is interchangeable with another. Physicians were told that if they pushed too hard they would be replaced by a different group of physicians willing to work for less. The concepts of quality, loyalty, past service to the institution were simply laughable.

The reason for all of the above was the almighty float (see *The Float*). Huge sums of money were taken by the HMOs and insurance companies in the form of premiums. This money was put to work earning money for them. The more they could delay the paying out of the money for services rendered, the more they could use it to generate additional income. Hence all of the games described above.

The formation of larger and larger groups of physicians to have more economic clout also meant a loss of independence for the physician and a diminishment of the entrepreneurial spirit that helped create the modern medical system we have today. Unfortunately, patients, in the main, have not helped. For savings of as little as ten dollars per month, patients will desert a physician with whom they have had a personal long-time relationship. So, to keep patients, physicians enter into contracts with HMOs, knowing full well that payments will be slow, disputed and in ever lower amounts. The era of solo practice is dead (there are still a few dinosaurs) and mass medicine has taken its place.

Present: It is really remarkable, as I reflect on medical care over seven decades, to see the changes that have taken place. In the beginning of my observations, medicine was relatively primitive and ineffective, but it was a true calling—a noble one at that. It had its flowering in the post-war years to, say, the early eighties. For a variety of reasons, some certainly attributable to the physicians themselves, the physician started to make the transition from professional to technician. The more tools they had, the more was expected of them. Patients started thinking of themselves as automobiles, taken into the super mechanic for repairs. Anything less than a perfect result was considered to be potentially malpractice. After all, they paid high premiums and high co-payments to the physicians—why shouldn't they have a perfect result? This feeling represents a conundrum. When physicians could do relatively little for the patient, they were held in high regard, since people knew the limitations of medicine. As medicine became more sophisticated and technological, physicians were able to do far more for patients than before, but at the price of less contact on a human level. Technology became a barrier to contact, as well as a powerful force for good. The explosion of knowledge leading to specialization and sub-specialization also diminished human contact, as the specialist would see the patient only briefly, and for a specific problem. Clearly a two-edged sword.

Another concept that produced a mixed result was the development of the revolt against authority. This was certainly not limited to physicians. One saw it in the revolt against teachers, police officers and other authority figures. As the population became better educated, and as the code words became independence and glorification of the self, physician judgment came to be questioned more and more. It seems certain that some physicians were too authoritarian and more than slightly smug. While it can be better to have an informed patient, such knowledge is of necessity limited, and may even be harmful. The Internet is a source of much information but little wisdom. The source for various treatment programs promoted on the Internet are often dubious, and unconfirmed, and as has been said before, knowledge in itself does not make for experience, skill and wisdom.

I therefore believe a new type of physician will emerge, but it will take several decades to become apparent. These individuals should be perfectly able to handle the complex knowledge that will be taught to them. However, they will be far more risk averse than their predecessors. They will not wish to start new practices, either de novo or by buying a retiring physician's practice. Rather they will become salaried employees of a large group. Regularity of hours will become important, and particularly for females who require regular, and at times limited hours so that they can attend to child bearing and child rearing. When I started medical school females constituted only a few percent of the class. Now, or shortly they will be in the clear majority. There will be no change in the quality of care, but the aggressiveness and entrepreneurial flair that built the current system will largely be over. Benefits will become very important and much discussed. Finally discussion will center continuously on the time to retirement and what will be done with retirement. This I witnessed in the VA and I am afraid it will become the norm for most physicians.

Not on Contingency

When I was in private practice, I would see a fair number of patients who were in auto accidents. They came to see me if they did not have any fractures or dislocations (in which case they would be under the care of an orthopedist) or any neurologic damage (in which case they would be under the care of a neurologist or neurosurgeon). I would be treating them for what is undoubtedly the most common form of injury in such cases, namely a soft tissue injury (an injury to the soft tissues of the musculoskeletal system: muscles, tendons, etc.) Indeed, even if the patient had the above-mentioned bone or nerve damage, they often would have soft tissue injuries as well which would need to be treated for full recovery. Some of the patients responded rapidly whereas others required an extended period of treatment, consisting of various physical therapy techniques, medications, local injections and the like. Because the treatment was often fairly prolonged and therefore expensive, I would not require payment in full until their case was settled (often after a period of several years) and then they would pay me just what they owed me. In effect, I was offering the patient an interest-free loan, guaranteed by them and their attorney that payment in full would be made after settlement. For many years that system worked and both patient and attorney would honor their agreement. I should mention that private insurance would not pay when there was litigation pending.

I did, of course, have patients who took advantage of the situation. One patient received her money and promptly declared bankruptcy so I could not collect the considerable amount of money she owed me. Several took the cash received from the settlement and promptly bought expensive furs, elaborate cruises, etc. and only then would they agree to pay me, over time, what they owed me. During this period, most attorneys made an effort to be sure that I was paid what was owed me.

All that changed over the last few years of my active medical practice days. After trial and settlement, the attorney would call and say that the settlement received was less than they expected. Therefore I would have to accept less than my full fee. If I didn't, they would not pay me at all or would drag payment out for months or even years. If I hired an attorney to go after them, I would have to pay the attorney and spend time going to court. My complaint that they had signed an agreement went unheeded. An agreement, even a signed agreement, was apparently not an agreement. My comment that I was not on a contingent basis as they were was greeted with a laugh. Mind you, if the patient (client) received more than what was expected, I obtained no benefit from that. There was no upside to the arrangement, only a downside. That was the end of a trusting relationship with my patients. Just one of many examples, unfortunately.

Patient Types

By this time in my career, I have seen enough new patients and done my fair share of initial evaluations, the history of physical examination (H&P). I do appreciate that at that time, much of the patient's behavior is due to nervousness and the process of sizing me up. However, in the course of performing the H&P, I am doing my own sizing up and have learned (for my own amusement) to categorize the various patient types.

The Diagnostician—This individual has honored me by permitting me to give him a second opinion. Armed with the *Merck Manual*, the *Physicians Desk Reference* (PDR) and opinions from friends and relatives, he has already established what is wrong. Woe to me if I should vary from his impression or offer my own differential diagnosis.

The Twofer—I have already completed my examination and am ready to institute my plan for work-up and treatment when this patient says, "As long as we're here," and starts telling me about a completely unrelated problem. In the last thirty seconds of her allotted time. With an office full of patients. With everyone looking at his or her watch and just waiting for me to be late.

The Distracter—I for one know that if I do not concentrate on what I am doing I will forget important parts of the exam. The distracter insists on discussing symptoms he left out of the history, other related health problems, the weather and people we know in common. I don't exactly have to go back to the beginning each time he speaks, but I feel as if I should.

The List Maker—When I see a patient walk into my consultation room clutching a sheaf of papers in her hand, I know I am in for trouble. The list consists of questions to be asked even before I have had a chance to do the H&P. "When am I going to be better?" usually starts the list, and it goes on from there.

The Record Keeper—This is a variant on the above. The patient walks in with a voluminous diary, spiral notebook or sheaf of papers handed to me with the comment, "I've kept this record for the past ten years to help you." Some help. It will take me an hour to read and then I will still have to take a history anyway.

"Of Course You Remember"—This patient tells me he was my patient ten years ago and has the same symptoms. "Of course you remember, don't you?" Sure I do. I have enough trouble remembering yesterday.

The Tangentialist—In perfect non-linear thought, the tangentialist will go from A to Z, without any stops in between. In response to a perfectly simple question which requires only a perfectly simple answer. How did we get from there to here? I wonder to myself.

The Fire Hydrant—The history comes out in a gush and under pressure, as if it must all be gotten in, before I have even had a chance to ask a single question. A variant is the Babbleonian—endless and disjointed speech in no particular order and unrelated to the question I must ask.

The Dramatist—Proudly proclaims, "Bet you've never seen anything like this before!" He's never seen it before. I've seen it dozens of times.

The Tooth Puller—No answer is freely given. I must ask several times in several different ways to extract an answer. I get the feeling that I am somehow in a test of wills. You would think that it was my health we were concerned about.

The Forgetter—Always just one more question. After I've left the examining room and with another patient.

The Influence Peddler—Wants me to know how important he is and what important people he knows. That should get him better faster.

The Expert Quoter—Reports to me that others know what is wrong with him. And who are these experts? Family. Friends. Neighbors. Why didn't he go to them for treatment?

The Parallel Drawer—My neighbor had the same problem, and she had this or that treatment. That makes it easy—if the neighbor indeed had the same problem, and this patient would respond in the same way. Both propositions extremely unlikely.

The Paper Chaser—Endless reams of paper brought in. For work. For attorney. For insurance company. For handicapped parking. For cancellation of trip. Etc. All to be done immediately, while he impatiently sits in the waiting room. Other patients? They don't really matter.

"It's an Emergency"—Patient squeezed in because it's an emergency. Symptoms found to be present for three months but there is indeed an emergency—patient is leaving town shortly and wishes to be cured post haste.

The Appointment Breaker—Repeated appointments broken at the last minute, leaving large gaps in the schedule. Often accompanied by the most imaginative excuses. Patient really wishes to be cured, but over the phone.

The Surrealist—"What is it?" "I don't know." "Will is get worse?" "If I knew I could tell you." "Can't you even give me a hint?" "You tell me what's wrong with you and I'll tell you what will happen." And so on.

The Wisher—"Doctor, just get me better." Shazam, you're better.

The Kiss of Death—"Doctor, I'm sure you can get me better. I've been to sixteen others and they have all failed" Sure I can.

124

Professional Fees

It was a fortuitous coincidence. I was busy filling out (on my own time) yet more forms and reports (gratis, of course) and guided by liberal notes from the patient (actually pages of computerized comments as well as urgings for me to "make the report strong") when I received an exquisitely detailed legal bill down to the tenth of an hour. Also included in the bill was a section labeled "costs" where what in my office would be considered normal operating costs were passed on to the client.

This set me to daydreaming. I imagined how my bill would look if I were to bill a patient in the style of an attorney and if I could turn office overhead costs into a profit center. Here is a month in the treatment of such a patient.

Actual Billing: 1.75 hours

Legal Style Billing Below:

BILLING DATE	ACTION	HOURS	COMMENT
3/1	Initial consultation	1.0	Patient in auto accident - typical soft tissue injury - no neurological deficit-no obvious bone pathology
3/1	Dictation of the consultation, writing of prescriptions, order for x-ray order for physical therapy, note for work for patient.	0.3	
3/1	Telephone call from patient re x-rays	0.1	Not yet read
3/1	Telephone call to radiologist	0.1	Slight abnormalities but not felt to be clinically relevant
3/1	Visit to x-ray department	0.3	x-rays reviewed because of the above abnormalities- agree with radiologist's conclusion
3/1	Telephone call from attorney	0.4	Promised me he needed only "2 minutes"; learned that attorney was retained **before** physician (first things first)-wanted to remind me that a "strong report" was necessary.
3/2	Telephone call from patient	0.1	Meds not yet working-should they be changed?
3/2	Long distance call to Seattle WA at insistence of patient	0.3	Uncle of patient- a psychoanalyst- wishes complete review of case and copies of all reports- reminds me that he was once a medical student too.
3/2	Telephone call from physical therapist	0.2	My orders all wrong – wishes to treat differently- will do so no matter what I say.
3/2	Discussion with secretary	0.1	Patient called- neighbor feels meds are all wrong.
3/2	New prescription written	0.1	

3/4	Filled out handicapped parking sticker. Letter written to excuse patient from work	0.2	
3/4	Telephone call from insurance carrier	0.2	Wants to know when patient will be better and ready to return to work- implies that my treatment all wrong- cousin had same problem and got better with different treatment.
3/6	Fill out form from insurance carrier	0.1	
3/8	Discussion with secretary	0.1	Patient called- nose itching- should meds be stopped? - recommended that they be continued a while longer.
3/8	Discussion with secretary	0.1	Patient wanted my diagnosis for itching nose- I suggested it might be related to pollen.
3/8	Discussion with secretary	0.1	Patient wants firm diagnosis- it is related to pollen!
3/15	Follow-up visit	0.25	First follow-up visit- discussion centered about my consultation report (thoroughly edited including grammar). Patient wished to add problems, which were not mentioned on the initial consultation- I agreed to an addendum. Patient wanted prescription for visit to acupuncturist, not previously discussed with me-various forms to fill out. Also examined patient and saw some improvement
3/15	Fill out forms and prescription for acupuncturist	0.3	Damage already done

3/15	Long distance call to Seattle	0.3	Call uncle at request of patient-three calls necessary before contact because he was busy (earning a living).
3/15	Family conference	0.3	Waylaid by spouse on way to restroom- full bladder surcharge imposed.
3/16	Discussion with secretary	0.1	Patient wishes to have a script for complete gym and Jacuzzi in basement as well as an outdoor pool- told secretary IRS is unlikely to pay for same
3/16	Script for gym, pool and Jacuzzi	0.1	Patient insisted
3/20	Follow-up visit	0.25	Patient admits to improving but not fast enough to permit ski trip. Wishes letter to airline for refund of ticket. Wants to know my opinion of herbal teas and manganese- have no opinion about them (get look which is a mixture of pity and contempt). Patient has lined up Orthopod, Neurologist and Neurosurgeon (ALL VERY BIG) if necessary
3/20	Letter to airline for cancellation of tickets	0.1	
3/20	Write orders for continuation of physical therapy	0.1	
3/21	Letter to insurance company	0.2	Wants full report including diagnosis, return to work date, etc.-refuses to make payment for services rendered. Treatment given to areas other than neck being reviewed because no mention was made in initial report- big hassle on the way.

3/26	Follow-up visit	0 25	Patient admits to improvement but bemoans loss of ski trip and other activities- I mildly suggest that life is not always fair and am rewarded with a dirty look. Discussion held by patient with uncle, non-M.D. neighbor and M.D. neighbor (Ob/Gyn) and all agree that MRI necessary
3/26	Script for MRI	0.1	Who am I to disagree with such a powerful line-up?
3/28	MRI report reviewed	0.1	Essentially normal with small midline bulge at C3-C4 with no impingement on cord
3/28	Telephone call from patient	0.2	Patient received report before I did- don't ask me how-panic- wishes to know about surgery- try to calm down but only partially successful
3/28	Fill out forms for insurance, work, etc.	0.25	
3/28	Review records- dictate medical (non- legal) report to attorney as requested	0.25	
3/28	Discussion with secretary	0.2	Patient willing to wait for half- hour while I dictated report and it was transcribed- told that I had an office full of patients but not terribly impressed. Finally agreed to give me 24 hours.
3/30	Telephone call from attorney	0.4	Outraged that I charged for report. I lightly suggested that attorneys do not take a deep breath without charging a client- did not think it funny- suggested that if settlement not large enough, I might not get full fee. I protested that I am not on a contingency fee basis-faint sneer heard- we negotiate.

Total Hours billed as legal billing: 7.5 hours

Costs To Me: Postage, fax, copying, long distance and local telephone calls, scheduling, drug refills, insurance filing, billing, confirming appointments, filling out forms.

And so it goes. But there is one element missing which would make the picture perfect. How about a retainer up front to pay for the cost of treatment? No messy billing, no write-offs, no dealing with insurance companies, collection agencies, etc. The daydream ended and I was back to filling out my forms.
(*Virginia Medical Quarterly*, Summer 1993)

Professional or Businessman?

The cry is often heard that physicians should be more businesslike. That is not an unreasonable proposition, at least on the surface, but it is a lot more complex and more difficult than it sounds.

On the face of it, physicians run a small business and should run it in a businesslike fashion. The truth, however, at least in the past, is that physicians did not see themselves as businessmen and did not really want to be businessmen. Their interests were quite different. They saw themselves as professionals who by circumstance were running a small business. There were exceptions, of course, individuals who were good at business and who enjoyed it, but it was not true in the main. This lack of interest, coupled with concentration on their medical practice, some naivete, and in some cases considerable arrogance (some felt that because they were bright, energetic and good at medicine they had transferable skills), made physicians frequent and well known marks for all sorts of get rich schemes which all too frequently failed—miserably. This does not imply an indifference to money on the part of physicians. Most felt that due to the level of education and training which they possessed, the difficulty of their job and the stress of their job, that a comfortable income from their work was not inappropriate. Few aspired to be among the mega-rich, at least from their occupation. If large sums of money were made, it was made from good investments, although as pointed out above, most physicians were not terribly skilled at that. Most physicians were dependent upon their office staff to run their business, and this not infrequently led to cases of embezzlement because physicians concentrated on their work and not their business.

In spite of what is said, patients also do not want physicians to be businessmen. They do not consider themselves merchandise and do not want to be considered as such. Rather they wish to be treated as individuals and strongly object when money is brought up in the context of their health. This has led to many patients considering the payment of their physicians as an option depending upon their current financial status, how they see themselves treated and what the result is of their treatment—whether they were or weren't cured. This in spite of the fact that no physician can guarantee a cure-only a best effort.

Unfortunately for everyone, medicine is becoming more and more of a business. In the past physicians could expect compensation for their services roughly comparable to what was felt in the community to be reasonable and usual. No longer. It is now a game played between the insurance company and the physician—the former to deny payment as long as possible and for as little as possible and the latter to do what is necessary to receive fair compensation for services rendered. To that end, physicians are joining together in larger and larger groups to be able to deal more effectively with the enormous insurance companies against whom, as individuals, they had no chance. This has meant the hiring of professionals to do battle with the insurance companies and if necessary the patients. Patients don't necessarily like this new arrangement but there is really nothing they can do about it. By joining a pre-paid health plan, presumably to save some money, they have given up a great deal of choice. No doubt physicians are conflicted about all of this. No doubt patients are conflicted about all of this. Nobody seems to be a happy camper.

The Invisible Web

Patients could never see it but there was an invisible web joining each physician with his group of referral doctors. It was of course to some degree based on friendship but also on hospital affiliation and most important of all knowledge of how the physician to whom the patient was referred performed. Although friendship and hospital affiliation certainly played a role, it was impossible to continually refer a patient to an incompetent physician or even to one with poor interpersonal skills if one wished to retain the patient. Therefore, on a long-term basis it was the performance of the physician to whom your patient was referred that counted. If he did well, you were thanked and praised. If he did not, you received the brunt of the complaints, probably lost the patient for good and had no good word of mouth referrals from that patient. A losing situation and one you were not likely to repeat.

It was even a more sophisticated web than that. You tried to match the needs of the patient, both medical and psychosocial, with the physician to whom you referred. Sometimes you wanted as the referral physician someone who was very aggressive, at other times very conservative. Sometimes the problem was straightforward and what you needed was someone with good technical skills. At other times you needed someone with good interpersonal skills. A difficult problem required someone who was very thorough and very insightful, while at other times you wanted someone who was a good psychological fit. It was also important to have someone with whom you personally could easily communicate so that there was a good exchange of ideas, and you were kept abreast of your patient's progress. Further, you would know the physician personally and be able to explain how he/she was likely to go about solving a problem. If the physician had certain foibles that could be explained in advance and the patient would be alerted. This was very comforting to the patient.

It is not like that at all now. You are now given a booklet with a list of those physicians participating in the plan held by the patient. It is possible that you know the physician to whom you will be referring, but it is equally possible that you know him/her only by name or not even know the physician at all. Then both you and the patient are taking a gamble.

The Way Things Were—A Reminder

Since my father was a physician, using the first floor of our home as his office (great for my father, not so felicitous for the family), I have been both an observer and participant in the medical scene over seven separate decades. The changes have been so enormous that it is difficult to remember the way medicine once was. To jog the memory of the older physicians and to inform the younger, here are some of the things that used to happen in medicine.

Discussions at various medical gatherings used to focus on interesting medical cases. Also discussed were family, recreation, vacations, investments, sporting events, politics, and the weather. You all know what is discussed now.

Physicians were proud to have their children express an interest in medicine as a career and thrilled when they were accepted into medical school.

Medical journals and medical meetings were devoted solely to advancements in medicine.

Hospital administrators at least pretended to listen to input from physicians.

Nobody was interested in your office medical chart but you. Doodles, the phone number of your garage mechanic and comments about the peculiarities of your patient could all be put on the chart with impunity.

Office charts and hospital charts were not the subjects of defensive charting. Written in haste and reviewed at leisure (with the benefit of 20/20 hindsight) was not even considered as a possibility.

Patients said, "Stupid, clumsy me" when their behavior produced an injury.

Prescription pads were kept where it was convenient for the physician, not where they were least likely to be stolen.

One attended medical meetings to gain knowledge, not CME credits.

The only professional contact with lawyers was settlement on your house and the making of a will.

Insurance companies assumed that four years of college (heavy in the sciences), four years in medical school and four to six years of post-graduate training better equipped the physician for medical necessity determinations than their billing clerk.

After the above noted training and its attendant sacrifices, the public assumed that physicians had something else in mind other than just gouging them for money. It was further assumed that income received was a result of hard, demanding work and not unearned and ill-gotten rewards.

Independent medical exams were just that—independent.

Like the rest of society, it was assumed that physicians were innocent until proven guilty and honest until proven otherwise.

Medical appointments were considered at least as important as a hair appointment or a golf starting time—one would no more likely break one than the other.

Patients came to you primarily for health problems, not the filling out of forms and the writing of reports. Patients listened to you about health care at least as much as to family and neighbors. Often they would actually follow your advice—go to the consultant you recommended, have the tests done that you ordered, fill the prescriptions you wrote.

Patients were re-evaluated at intervals felt to be appropriate by the treating physician and not by the insurance company.

Gifts from pharmaceutical detailers such as pens, key chains, reflex hammers, penlights and other rapidly lost or broken gifts were seen as a simple thank-you for giving your time to them, not as a bribe and not a cause for moral anguish.

There was no relationship between outcome and payment, absent gross negligence. It was understood by patients that you did the best you could but that you could not solve all problems. The current idea of perfect care leading to a perfect outcome (provided cheaply) would have been incomprehensible.

It was considered an honor and not a burden to treat fellow physicians and their families.

When asked at a social event what you did for a living, you were proud to say that you were a physician. You did not have to prepare yourself psychologically for the verbal onslaught of snide comments.

You never once thought about how some action of yours would appear when you were on the witness stand.

You were not second-guessed on treatment by a disembodied telephone doctor who reviewed the chart but never saw the patient. (In vain I have pleaded for those voices to "cut out the middleman"—me—and treat the patient directly—via telephone, of course).

The patient was considered to be one person and all records were kept in one chart. Now each health problem that is covered by a separate insurance company is kept in a separate chart.

This is the way some of the things were in medical practice. Change is normal and natural; however, are all of the changes detailed above really for the better?
(*Virginia Medical Quarterly*, Winter 1993)

"You're Always Late"—Why Physicians Are Sometimes Late

It's something of a cliché. The subject of cocktail humor and late night TV humor, with a certain sense of bitterness underlying the jokes. Physicians are always late with their appointments. That surely explains why patients don't pay their bills. Those telling the jokes of course are never, never late with their own business appointments. Of course.

In actuality it is indeed sometimes the fault of the physicians. Some indeed grossly overbook. Some are completely oblivious to the passage of time. Some do not have the discipline to attempt to keep to a schedule. Some are insensitive to the needs of their patients.

In the majority of cases, however, it is not in actuality the fault of the physicians. Most physicians overbook to some extent. The reason for that is that all too often patients simply fail to show. If there is an occasional follow-up appointment for which a patient fails to show the time can certainly be put to good use with other work that always needs to be done. If, however, one or more new patient appointments as well as a few follow-up appointments are not filled, that puts big holes in the physician's schedule. Since the only thing that he has to sell is his time (and with it his expertise) serious dents in his capacity to earn a living are at stake. Hence physicians anticipate this and tend to overbook to some degree to compensate for this. I have always said that patients show more respect for their golf starting time or hair dressing time than their physician's appointments. They would not think of not calling if they had to cancel one of those things. And the excuses one hears. The appointment card gave the wrong date. If you ask to see it they somehow forget. The dog ate the card. And so on. And so on.

Although appointments are booked at regular intervals, say fifteen minutes for a follow-up appointment, forty-five minutes for a routine new appointment, one hour for an extended new appointment, etc., human problems do not come in such neat compartments. Some problems can be solved in only a very few minutes whereas others take much longer. Some people are considerate of the physician's time whereas others wish to get full value for their money, oblivious to the demands that they are putting on the physician's time. Sometimes unexpected problems spring up during what seemed to be a routine appointment. Emergencies must somehow be squeezed in. Phone calls from the hospital or from other physicians or from the lab must somehow be answered. Physician's offices are hectic places and some allowances must be made for that.

I personally made every effort to try to keep as close to the schedule as humanly possible, being aware of the attitude of patients towards my being on time. On one occasion—and only on one occasion—when I was (gasp) fifteen minutes late, the patient demanded an explanation. When I told him that I make every effort to keep a schedule but occasionally things happen beyond my control, he stormed out of the office. Although some people never understood, thankfully most did. I don't know how I could have practiced if they did not.

Miscellanea Medica

House Staff Days

A house staff is composed of those physicians who are employed by a hospital, usually a part of or affiliated with a medical school, and who trade their labor for additional education and training. When I was a house staff officer, we had interns, residents and a few fellows. Interns had their medical degree (they could now legitimately be called doctor) but could not practice medicine until they had completed their year of internship. Residents were eligible to practice medicine but chose to get additional training in a specialty. Fellows were rare and were those who completed their residency but who wished additional very specialized training. Nowadays internships and residencies are combined and are designated Post Graduate Year (PGY) I, II, etc. Fellowships are far more common now with the burgeoning of very highly specialized areas of medicine and surgery.

It was a time for the assuming of progressively more and more responsibility in the care of the patient. By the time one was a chief resident, one had essentially complete responsibility for the care of the patients on the service, with the advice and supervision of the attending physicians. As a medical student, I had zero responsibility for patient care, with one exception. When I rotated through Obstetrics at the city hospital, I was told by the

139

harried resident to go into the Delivery Room and perform a delivery, something I had never done before. The only instruction I had was "Don't drop the baby!" The fact was that the patient involved was a grand multipara (one who had delivered five or more children) and she in effect delivered herself. Then a nurse came in and helped with the afterbirth, and I was initiated into the mysteries of childbirth.

When I started my internship, I took what was known as a rotating internship: four months on a surgical service, four months on a medical service and two months each on pediatrics and obstetrics/gynecology. A few, who were sure what they wished to do after internship took either a straight medical or straight surgical internship. In retrospect, I am glad that I was exposed to the various disciplines, their diseases and their problems, although I would not have direct use for most of them. I do recall that after I had completed my pediatrics rotation and moved on to obstetrics/gynecology, I found a mother in labor who had a peculiar rash which was disturbing to the whole delivery suite staff. I immediately saw what it was—chicken pox, which threw everybody into a further tizzy as to what to do.

Our compensations as interns was $60 per month that came, after deductions, to a biweekly check of $22. We were immediately told by older physicians that we were paid too much, as they had gone through their internship with no pay at all. We did of course get room, board and laundry. When I had my first residency posting, I was told that my monthly stipend would be $180, and I recall my initial reaction—"What am I going to do with all that money?" That reaction did not last very long, of course. We made do with the money because we had to and because of the hours we worked. We were on call for thirty-six hours and had twelve hours off. We worked every other weekend, which meant that we entered the hospital on Saturday morning and did not emerge until Monday evening at six. When we had a weekend off, we started our time off at noon on Saturday and returned on Monday morning. Not too much time to get in trouble or even to spend money. I do not mean to imply that we went completely without sleep when we were on call, but it was frequently interrupted sleep. Fortunately our hospital had a relatively quiet emergency room, with relatively few admissions and thus we were able to get some rest. Those who chose internships at busier hospitals had far more work—and far less rest.

At that time, we interns rode the ambulance on its calls. Initially it was fun to see us zipping by traffic (at that time people pulled over when they heard an ambulance coming), but it soon became a bore, although not without some humor. One night, when on ambulance call, I was awakened and rode for what seemed like an eternity to find a potential patient under a very dim lamppost. He then told me he had something in his eye and wanted me to take it out—then and there. He received a tongue lashing from me and we returned to the hospital where I tried to complete my night's rest. At another time I was a hero, at least according to the *New York Daily News*, where my name and picture were on the back page of the paper. A young boy was fished out of an icy pond into which he had fallen (he was luckier than his friend who drowned). My role in the heroic rescue? When he was put in the ambulance I put a blanket on him. At yet another time I received an ambulance call while sleeping, got dressed, grabbed the ambulance bag and waited downstairs in the lobby to be picked up. When the ambulance did not arrive, I called the operator, who told me she did not call me—I had dreamed it. Nowadays it is done with far more skill and precision by fully trained Emergency Medical Technicians (EMTs) who are part of the fire departments.

We had suffered humiliation as medical students, particularly with some departments who felt (1) it was the proper way to teach and (2) they could, so they did. It was surprising, after we received our medical degree, to see some of these practices continue. Not by everyone, of course, but enough. As newly minted interns, we were told by the administrator in no uncertain terms that he could get all the house officers he wanted but nurses were in short supply, so if we had an altercation with a nurse it would be we who would go. Great for our ego as newly minted M.D.s. Besides, who wanted to fight with the nurses? We wanted to go out with them. When on the pediatrics service, we came in contact with the department chief, a very short chief with a very large Napoleon complex. He took great delight in humiliating us if we failed to know the answer to his questions, to the acute embarrassment of the attending physicians on rounds with us. Most of us were simply rotating through pediatrics and had no intention of entering the field. We were glad when that rotation ended.

The biggest problem then, and in subsequent years in residency was with the surgeons. Again, not all surgeons, but the behavior of some that I witnessed was astonishing. In my very first week of internship I was on a surgical rotation, and was on my way to scrub in when I got a call to go to the Emergency Room. I made the decision that that was more important, took care of the problem and then proceeded to the Operating Room where I received one of the worst tongue-lashings I had ever taken, even after explaining why I was late. My sole job in the O.R. was to hold the retractors that could easily have been done by someone else, but the surgeon was king and he was not going to be inconvenienced by anyone or anything. In subsequent residency years I observed and felt even worse behavior on the part of some surgeons. I was not very gently bumped with the belly of a surgeon of some girth and had my knuckles rapped with an instrument by a surgeon who felt that I was not paying sufficient attention. My job was to hold retractors and I couldn't even see the operating field so I don't see how I could pay attention. I saw a surgeon throw instruments about the O.R. and heard others scream at the nurses, berate the anesthesiologists and in general make damn fools of themselves. This type of behavior would not be tolerated today.

It could be said that although a few, a very few, were independently wealthy, most of us shared genteel poverty. We made do with what we had. Recreation was at public parks or beaches. We ate out occasionally at the most inexpensive of restaurants, and occasionally went to the movies. The truth is, we had very little free time and we were usually too tired to fully enjoy it even then. Our energies in the hospital were directed to the work at hand but that did not stop us from making wry comments about our superiors, the administrators, the patients, the nursing staff, etc. Our interests were circumscribed by the hospital and its goings on with very little concern about the outside world. At one institution there was a Sunday night ritual where all available house staff gathered to watch the television show *Maverick*. Following that we adjourned to the kitchen where any food that was found in the hospital refrigerators was ours to eat. I recall one time gorging on Maraschino cherries and another time—would you believe—on mayonnaise. That practice was ended by the administration when some of the married house staff used the occasion to stock up on staples for their family.

I did House Staff time on both coasts, and did not see a great deal of difference in the workings of hospitals on either coast, with one exception. Remember, this was the fifties I am talking about. On the East Coast I could never remember an attending physician making hospital rounds in any garb but a suit and tie. Early in my days on the West Coast, I positively gasped when I saw, on a Sunday, a medical attending enter the elevator to make rounds in his tennis clothes. I personally never got beyond making rounds in a sport coat with a sport shirt, even in the far more relaxed eighties and nineties. One thing that was the same on both coasts was the training of nurses to rise when a physician entered the nurse's station. We all tried to sneak onto the station behind their backs so they would not have to rise. That training soon departed, along with the wearing of caps that signified which school they had graduated from, a source of great pride to many. Now one enters the nursing station with the nurses totally oblivious to your presence.

I did not observe a great deal of horseplay at the various hospitals I had worked at although I had heard about it at other institutions. I do recall that during my rotation through Obstetrics I had both hands occupied while assisting in a delivery. The resident slipped around, undid my scrub pants and then called all the nurses to the viewing window behind me to see me in my shorts with my pants around my feet, to my acute embarrassment.

As I soon found out, pay at the hospital during residency training was inadequate for even the most basic of things such as owning a car, taking your two weeks of vacation, minimal entertainment, etc. This was brought out to me when I saved for months to buy a ten-year old car previously owned, I was assured, by a spinster schoolteacher from Pasadena. This contrasted with what I saw one morning while going to patient rounds. A fairly new Cadillac pulled up and out stepped, in uniform, the maid who cleaned my room. Most of us therefore had to supplement our incomes by moonlighting, that is working during the evening or at night once or twice a week or on weekends at a medical clinic somewhere in town. It was distasteful work at best. We were tired because we worked the full day before our evening or night shift and would have to work a full day the next day as well. Some of the clinics were better than others but some were simply patient mills, where one ground out the patients as fast as they came in. One clinic had no chairs in the waiting room to better accommodate the mob, and we were alerted to the number of patients in the waiting room by a series of colored light bulbs, each color representing the number of patients waiting. When the red light went on, we were at maximum capacity and had to put on our track shoes to get through. Each patient visit was concluded by an intravenous injection of niacin that gave them a nice flush but had no medical benefit. I suspect some of them came precisely for that. It did them no harm but I gave it only with the greatest of reluctance. I was very idealistic then.

House staff days were a mixed blessing. At times the work was fascinating and at times deadly dull. The hours were long and hard. Some of the work was pleasant and some extremely distasteful. However, I learned what I needed to learn to be able to practice my profession and that is what counts.

John

He was a force of nature and the most unforgettable person I have ever met. Our relationship spanned over a quarter of a century, and had some ups and more than enough downs. There were very few times when things were calm and quiet.

I was stuck in the middle of a Residency training program in which the chief of service was more interested in thinking about retirement than in training us. We essentially fended for ourselves with less than spectacular results. Much of the teaching was to have been done by a professor in our specialty at a nearby university with which our department was affiliated, but unfortunately he came to learn rather than to teach. It was a case of the halt leading the blind, and we suffered as a result of it.

Then we heard that John was coming, and his arrival was greeted with great curiosity as some of his story leaked out. He was a tall and distinguished Englishman who apparently had an illustrious father, one who was a well-known and published physician. When we first met John he positively exuded self-confidence and was very open with us—to an astonishing, almost embarrassing, degree. For example, in short order he told us that during World War II, as a physician, he had eighteen different postings. In some they barely let him in the gate, saying that his reputation preceded him and he was to be posted elsewhere forthwith. This was told to us without the faintest hint of shame or embarrassment.

After the war, he went to New Zealand but he left shortly (he was never clear about the reason) and then took up private practice in Richmond, VA. He lost no time in telling the referring physicians how abysmally ignorant they were. He did appear to be faintly puzzled as to why they stopped referring patients to him, but as would be expected in short order his practice failed. He then took an orthopedic residency, completed it, but had a fight with the Chief of Service and was denied eligibility to take the Boards to be certified in the specialty. He then fell back on his original specialty and requested Board certification status on the basis of his training in England. Unfortunately, he had a fight with the powerful chairman of the specialty board. To pay penance he was required to take an additional year of training, and that is how he came to be among us.

It wasn't long before he noted that we were learning little or nothing, and he took us under his wing. He did not hesitate to tell the Chief how poor the training was, and a mutual, cordial dislike was established. However, we, the residents, gained enormously as he took over the teaching. Although more than slightly dogmatic, he taught us fundamentals upon which we could build. My future specialty interests were clearly shaped by John and what he taught us.

Our paths parted after completion of residency training, but we would meet occasionally at medical meetings or conferences. He had written a textbook which was well received, and he was working on another. He passed Part I (the written part of the Boards), but when it came to Part II (the oral part) he ran into trouble. When asked what medical articles he had recently read, he informed his examiners that he did not read—he wrote. He thereupon flunked Part II of the Boards and was required to take them again. He took a position as Chief of Service at a VA hospital in California. He peppered the Central Office of the VA with complaints about the staff, the waste, and the inadequacy of the programs, indeed everything–so they responded by abolishing his job. He was, however, able to land another job in Philadelphia, not too terribly far from where I was living and working, in Washington, D.C.

That last fact was important because at the time I had a burning desire to write a textbook myself. A previous co-author of mine backed out after month upon month of desultory discussions and false starts, and I knew that at that stage of my professional life, I would not be able to do the job by myself. John was the logical choice. He was in my specialty. He had a wealth of knowledge. He was a published author. He lived relatively nearby. We knew each other. I knew the problems he had had but felt that they could be overcome. In hindsight, there was no question that I was blinded to reality by my overwhelming desire to write the book.

Although we signed an agreement to joint authorship of the book, we had nothing at all in the way of an outline. It was completely inchoate. The agreement was signed in the spring but it was not until the fall that we were able to get together in what became the usual fashion—I would go to him—at his convenience. We chatted, had dinner, talked in general terms about the book but never even put in motion anything specific on which we could work. He did, however, inform me of two interesting things. First, he signed a contract with the publisher for another book, and that would take precedence over our joint book. Second, he was moving back to California at the end of the year. It is obvious that I should have cut my losses then, but I did not.

In December, by coincidence, I was flying out of Philadelphia, and I thought it would be our last chance in a long while to talk face to face, develop a rough outline and permit me to get started while he was doing his own thing. This he had agreed to do. However, when I got to Philadelphia, I received no answer to repeated phone calls. Much later, and with absolutely no embarrassment, he informed me that he had gone to the Ice Capades that night even though he knew that I was coming.

Approximately two years passed without anything being accomplished. He then told me that it was his concept of a collaboration that we should each write separately (mind you, we had no outline) and submit our work separately to the publisher. Shortly thereafter, with great fanfare, he announced that he had completed his part of the book and was about to submit it to the publisher. I was horrified but through flattery and cajoling (I did suggest to him that at the very least I would be an interested reader) I was able to get him to send the MSS to me for review. My heart sank when I sat down to read the MSS. It was terrible. I called him and begged him not to submit it. He did submit it, without my knowledge or permission (I was the senior author), and it was promptly rejected. Back to square one.

Time passed. No apology was forthcoming. We met infrequently, usually at medical meetings. Here is what it was like at the meetings, where we arranged to discuss the book and plot how to proceed further. He would perform a slow parade from the meeting rooms to his own room, meeting and chatting with people on the way. Once in his room, he would make a few telephone calls and then we would talk about the book, getting absolutely nowhere. Shortly afterward he would jump up and state that he had to go to this or that lecture, and was out of the room before I could say anything. Fortunately, at one of these meetings, I had an inspiration for an outline of the book that would permit us to proceed with the writing. We divided assignments and went our separate ways.

More time passed. Some work was accomplished. It was time for us to get together and compare notes—something he didn't want to do but it was apparent, at least to me, that it had to be done. As usual, I went to visit him, this time in California. For that I took two weeks of annual leave. He did not want to waste annual leave so we would work together but only during evenings and weekends. He expected me to work all day, and became quite annoyed if I took time off to relax. Surprisingly, once we started working, we worked very closely, and it was very stimulating, even exciting, to see something take shape. So much so that I became anxious to continue.

On one occasion John came to visit and stay with us. He informed us that on several occasions he had been in Washington, D.C. but that he had not bothered to call me, let me know how he was doing with the work, etc. It should be noted that he was more than mildly parsimonious so initially all expenses such as long distance calls were made by me. At any rate, he did honor us by his presence this once, and fortunately never again. After apparently seeing Monty Woolley in "The Man Who Came to Dinner," he decided to play the role to the hilt. With great grace and aplomb, he had us waiting on him hand and foot. It was truly a relief to have him gone.

Work progressed apace. Surprisingly all the writing was complete. He graciously let me do all the hard work—indexing, editing, references, photos, permission slips, etc. Incidentally he had an interesting idea about references. There should be none. This in a medical textbook. Fortunately the editors told him that there would be references, and he again graciously let me do all the work obtaining them. In a way I was grateful since I knew that the job would get done in a reasonably timely fashion. Once in the hands of editors, an enormous amount of re-editing (these were the days before computers) and other related tasks were performed and—would you believe it—the book actually became published, nearly ten years after we first discussed it.

Nearly another decade passed. The book was more than reasonably successful. John and I remained on good terms–even better than before, and I started thinking about a second edition. I will never forget the scene. I was in the office of my editor and my publisher–both of whom I had gotten to know fairly well. They had also published John's three prior books and knew him very well indeed. Both of them told me quite frankly that I was crazy to consider writing another book with him. He was impossible to deal with. They also told me that all the MSS that he had submitted were so bad that they were essentially rewritten by a junior editor. On and on they went. To this day I can still hear my response: "I think he has changed." So the contract was signed and the process was started all over again.

The pattern remained completely the same. All collaboration was on his terms, at his convenience and at his location—whether at his home or wherever he might be lecturing. Each contact brought about condescension on his part and relatively little in the way of accomplishment. By this time I was a lot more knowledgeable and a lot more confident, so that I did not hesitate to disagree with him. A do or die meeting was set for my house. On the day of the meeting, a phone call announced that he would not be coming. Shortly thereafter I received a note

151

in which he relinquished all rights to the book. I completed it myself.

How to sum up my relationship with John? It was obviously complex. I respected his medical knowledge and was grateful that he shared it with me. With all the problems, a text was indeed finally published. Knowing him has produced a wealth of incredible situations and incredible stories. The only word to adequately describe him was the word of both the editor and the publisher–impossible. If it were possible would I ever write with him again? NO! On the other hand . . .

Justice

I had sold my practice and, approximately two weeks before the turnover, I learned that one of my receptionists was going to be fired when the transition was complete. She was an older woman who had been hired about a year previously. I felt that I was obligated to tell her so that she could begin to make plans. She was single and had to work, as she had no other means of support. I was shocked when, instead of thanking me for the warning, she picked up her purse and stormed out of the office. We tried to get in touch with her for two or three days to find out if she planned to return to work but when we were unsuccessful, we hired a young girl who had been inquiring about the position. After all, the work still had to be done. We were again shocked when about a week later the older woman called and said she planned to return to work. We then told her regretfully that we had not heard from her and that we therefore hired someone else.

My third shock came a month or two later when I found out that I was in the process of being sued on the basis of age discrimination! The suit was being handled (investigated) by the Equal Employment Opportunity Commission. I then hired a lawyer who took her fee, listened to my story and informed me of the undying principle that no good deed goes unpunished. She then wrote a letter to the Commission explaining the facts.

Time passed and ultimately the case was dismissed for lack of merit. For the plaintiff there was no cost involved and possible financial benefit could have accrued if the case was successful. For me there was aggravation, consumption of time as well as the payment of significant legal fees. Had the loser been forced to pay court costs and all legal fees, in all likelihood there would have been no suit at all, since there was no justification for it in the first place. Justice certainly seems to be lacking in our current legal system.

Marching Towards Mediocrity

I have served in various governmental medical facilities—some terrible and some satisfactory. My service in the Veterans Administration hospital system (VA) approximates the middle of governmental medicine and I believe foreshadows what will be the future with all of American medicine.

Perhaps the VA has changed but I can only record what it was like when I did my residency training there. There was constant discussion before, during and after my residency service about abolishing the VA hospital system entirely since the level of care was deemed to be less than acceptable. One compromise that was worked out was that each VA hospital was affiliated with a nearby medical school. I believe that that was of some help. Nevertheless, problems galore remained.

Some of the VA medical staff were involved in teaching, both at the VA hospital where medical students and residents rotated, as well as at the university itself. Others were involved in research both at the VA and the university. In this sense, they functioned as would any physicians in academic medicine. It was in the area of patient care that I saw vast differences between what they, the VA physicians did, and what I would later find out was the life of a physician in the private practice of medicine.

At the VA, a high premium was placed on regular hours. After hours the patient was the responsibility of the duty officer. Even during the regular working hours there was no emphasis on hard work. The day started in the coffee shop, there was a lengthy lunch break and the last hour or so was spent in conversation and watching the clock until it was time to go home. The overwhelming number one topic of conversation was the amount of time left until retirement, and what would be done once retired. I am not talking about short termers with only months to go before retirement. I am talking about those who had many years to go before eligible for retirement. Much of the workday was concentrated on personal interests such as research or writing, rather than on patient care.

Life was very different in private practice. The workday ended when the work ended. If you had to come in early or stay late then you did so. If you were too busy to sit down for lunch, then so be it. Meetings were often held at night because it was impossible to fit in all of the meetings during the day. And you went. Most private practice physicians were willing to do whatever it took to earn a living. It was felt that one had twenty-four-hour seven-day-a-week responsibility for the patient. Of course one would share evening and weekend call, cover for each other during vacations and out of town meetings, but the sense of responsibility was still there. Finally, I never until the most recent past heard any discussion of retirement. Most people really enjoyed doing what they were doing. I think it fair to say that the brightest, most motivated, hardest working and most innovative physicians went into private practice.

VA care was not bad, nor was it great. I think it fair to say it produced mediocrity. During my last years of practice and from what I have heard since, private practice is also marching towards mediocrity. The habits of the VA are becoming the habits of the private practice world. Also, the best and the brightest are not going into medicine, but are turning their talents elsewhere. These trends are long-term and will not become apparent for decades. Their effects will be devastating on the type of care received.

Medical Liability: If You Win, You Still Lose

As far as I can tell, the modern plague of personal liability suits started with actions against physicians approximately a quarter century ago. It is not exactly an honor one would brag about, but I do believe it is so. Of course, liability existed before that. I recall that when I was a resident in the late 1950s, we the hospital house staff were informed by the administration that we had to have liability insurance. We resented it but there was nothing we could do, and so for the sum of thirty-five dollars per annum, we were insured. Up until then I had

155

never heard about a physician being sued for malpractice, and for the next two decades that situation persisted. Then the deluge began, and has persisted until the present time.

Let me say on the outset that physicians should not be immune from the consequences of their actions, and the actions of some physicians at some times are truly inexcusable. Further, patients deserve fair and just compensation for any harm visited upon them. However, the problem is far more complicated than would seem on the surface.

It should be understood that mistakes are part of the human condition, and nobody is immune from them. These mistakes can be of commission, or more commonly, of omission. Good and conscientious physicians make them as do those few who seem to always be in trouble. Also an adverse outcome is not necessarily the result of negligence or malpractice. Unfortunately, it may happen beyond anyone's control. The question then arises as to how to treat chronic malefactors, what system of justice is best suited to handle problems as they arise, and how do we go about trying to prevent problems from happening in the future. I submit that the current system of torts, i.e. handling the problem through the courts is expensive, wasteful and the least likely to set off what is needed—a continuous cycle of progressive improvement in care and a lessening in the number of mistakes. I managed to go through an entire lifetime of practice without the trauma of being sued, but I just consider myself extremely fortunate, and I shudder when I hear the stories about what others go through. I have also testified and given depositions on behalf of other physicians and can only say that there but for the grace of God go I.

The first question to ask is why individuals choose to go into medicine in the first place. The same question is true of course for all of the health professions. The immediate cynical answer is to get rich but that is truly far off the mark. Individuals choose the health professions out of a genuine desire to help other people. For that they are willing to make an extraordinary sacrifice of time and energy, both in training and afterwards. Therefore the onset of a lawsuit is not seen as simply the cost of doing business in the U.S. today. Nor is it seen as a means of extraction of money from what is viewed as an individual with deep pockets, or a result of bad relations or a simple act of revenge, but as an attack on the very raison d' être of the physician/healer. This causes extraordinary pain. Self-flagellation inevitably follows, as does sleeplessness, guilt and self-doubt. Enormous amounts of time are consumed as the case wends its way through the court system. Meetings with attorneys, conferences of all sorts, depositions and sometimes a trial consume the life of the physician under suit. Often, the lawyer assigned by the insurance company does not have the physician's best interests at heart (he may rather be primarily concerned with the interests of the insurance company that hires him, making judgments based on their needs rather than those of the physician). Often that makes it necessary for the physician defendant to hire his own attorney with money out of his own pocket.

If the case goes to trial, the physician's supposed sins are trotted out for all to see. That is the way our adversary system works. The opposing lawyer tears into the physician's credibility. Opposing experts castigate the physician's judgment, skill and anything else that can be brought up. The plaintiff takes the stand and portrays the physician as a monster. If judged guilty, life will go on but not without cost. If judged innocent, the defendant will still feel guilty and will be scarred. It may come as a surprise to some but there are widespread support groups to help physicians who have been sued to deal with the psychological problems of the lawsuit, no matter how the suit comes out.

How will physicians (those who have been sued and those who know about it) behave in the future? It is terribly sad and unfortunate that relationships with patients undergo a subtle change. They are seen not simply as people in need but as potential enemies. One must guard what one says. One must make copious notes with the idea that someone in the future may be judging one's actions, based on those notes. One must order tests for self-protection even though one knows from experience that they will come back negative. I confess to mixed behavior on that score, depending upon how I feel that day. One day I will say, the hell with it, I will do what I think is right and damn the consequences. On other days I say, why take risks and put my career and me in jeopardy. Just order everything in sight, even if you know that it is not necessary. Finally, many physicians say, why did I choose medicine as a profession in the first place? I don't need the long and demanding hours, the enormous sacrifice of time, energy and money in my education and my training only to put myself through all of this. Of course some physicians manage to take it (all that is entailed in a lawsuit) in course and brush it off, but I believe that the majority of physicians do not.

What, then, can we do to fairly compensate the patient for any harm done, get rid of the few bad apples who plague the rest of us and permit an open and frank discussion of changes necessary to lessen mistakes in the future? I believe the patient's best interests would be served by a no-fault system in which an outside panel of physicians and lawyer, a judge or even a trial lawyer acting as an arbitrator could, as best as possible, affix what would be appropriate compensation for the plaintiff. This would be cheaper, faster and more just than the current system, which is akin to a crapshoot. If you win you get the jackpot, and if you lose you get nothing. The next problem is getting rid of the few bad apples who unfortunately are among us. Although some physicians are falsely accused by their colleagues for a variety of reasons (personal conflicts, jealousy, and venality) the problem is how to deal with those who are truly bad apples. Removing a physician from the hospital staff is an exceedingly difficult and frustrating business. It consumes an enormous amount of time and is likely to be countered by a lawsuit by the affected physician claiming a variety of abuses by the medical staff. As I mentioned, a few of these claims are valid but most are simply a deflection of blame or an attempt to gain financial reward from the hospital, medical staff or anyone else felt to be a likely candidate for a law suit and a large compensation. There is a large national practice database kept by the Health Resources Service Administration of the Department of Health and Human Services. I think it fair that criminal activity, removal of state licensure and removal of medical staff privileges are appropriate entries in such a database. However, unsubstantiated claims by patients, lawsuits in which the defendant was not found guilty, lawsuits that were settled out of court and any other items are not fair items in such a database. Currently such information is not available to the public but is available to the industry, namely hospitals, insurance companies, etc. There is a movement afoot (a constant phenomenon) to make such information available to the public. In my view, that would be akin to making raw FBI files which include all sorts of unsubstantiated charges available to the public.

Finally, and most important, there should be a mechanism in place for physicians to be evaluated in a non-judgmental fashion, so that it can be a non-threatening learning experience. All of us can benefit, and learn, from mistakes made in the course of work. These mistakes happen to each and every one of us, and the atmosphere should be that of a process of lifelong learning, not of punishment. There are many ways this can be done, but perhaps the best way is that of chart review, both in the hospital and in the office. Physicians themselves will have to pay for the cost of this, but it is after all not only an educational experience but a help in avoiding future legal liability. Admission of mistakes in the hospital setting should be for educational and not punitive purposes. Medical liability as it is now constructed is a flawed system which consumes all too much time and money (physicians have told me—at least those in the high risk professions—that they have to work many months of the year just to pay their liability insurance) and is really not the best way to further educate physicians and improve their performance.

Memories of a Medical Career

It is now forty-seven years since my graduation from medical school and I have reached the end of my medical career. I started medical school only a short time after the end of WWII, and therefore have been witness to what can only be seen as astonishing changes in medicine—in the tools available as well as and in the delivery of care. Because these changes have been dramatic but have occurred gradually, it is only by forcing oneself to look back that the magnitude of the changes becomes apparent.

Two instances during medical school days stand out to show the differences between then and now. The first was on a medical service, the second on a surgical service. During the weekly medical grand rounds, the Chief of Medicine, the attending physicians, the senior and junior medical residents, the interns, the senior and junior medical students all gathered in amazement to look at the "chair treatment" for myocardial infarction. Popularized by Samuel Lavine, M.D. of Boston, a patient was actually allowed to sit in a chair after two weeks of bed rest, rather than the previously demanded three weeks of bed rest during which the patient did not move a muscle. It was revolutionary. Now, patients with myocardial infarctions, if vital signs are stable, dangle at the side of the bed that day, walk within seventy-two hours and are discharged from the hospital after one week.

The second instance occurred when I was a senior medical student and was permitted to stand out of the way of the surgeons, in the back of the operating room, while they performed their very first mitral commissurotomy—the manual splitting of the valves of the chambers between the left atrium and the left ventricle which had grown together as a result of rheumatic fever. The drama in the operating room was palpable. Within a decade this was a procedure which was relegated to the senior resident as surgeons advanced towards cardiac transplant surgery and implantation of mechanical hearts, something undreamed of then but relatively commonplace now.

161

It is difficult to imagine how one practiced medicine before such a wide range of sophisticated diagnostic tools in every specialty became available; and before such a broad therapeutic armamentarium with which to treat the problem, once diagnosed. If true of outpatient office medicine it was even truer for hospital medicine, with space-aged tools for both diagnosis and treatment available. One would think that with these advances physicians would be beside themselves with joy at what they could accomplish. In actuality, from my observations, gloom and unhappiness pervade the profession of medicine.

There is a palpable difference between the conversations of physicians then and now. Whatever the words before, the background music was upbeat. Yes, there were problems galore. Yes, there was petty bickering and politicking and back stabbing, but one still had the feeling that things were far better than worse, that whatever our specialty, we were all in medicine together with a shared sense of camaraderie and of mission, that we were part of an elite but an elite that was trained to serve. The conversations now are all a dirge with virtually everyone feeling that the problems far outweigh the benefits. I have heard what I had never heard before—young physicians saying that if they knew before they stated what they know today they would never have gone into medicine; older physicians counting down the days until retirement; those in-between planning alternative careers or ways to take early retirement. All is not trouble of course, but a telling example of the change is the way announcements by physicians to their peers of the entrance of a child into medical school is made. Before, the proud parent was heartily applauded and there was much merriment and back-slapping. Now the scene is quite different. After the announcement is made, questions like, "Did you try to explain it to him?" or "Is she aware of what lies ahead?" are answered in a somewhat sheepish tone by "I tried to explain but he wouldn't listen," or, "She'll have to find out for herself."

How does one account for the dramatic technological advances leading (in most cases) to an improved quality and length of life and the growing discontent among physicians? Again I should emphasize that not every day is filled with doom and gloom and not every physician is unhappy with his lot, but a clear change in attitude amongst the majority of physicians has taken place from the beginning of my career to the present. The question is, "Why?" Also, what does it mean for the future of medicine and the future of health care for this country?

From an historic perspective, medical training was a catch as catch can thing until the (Abraham) Flexner report around the turn of the twentieth century brought about a dramatic change in medical and post-graduate training; however, until World War II those physicians who wanted the best and most advanced post-graduate training went to various European centers. After World War II to the present time, the United States has been the center for medical advances and medical and post-graduate training. Whether this will continue is problematic for a number of reasons.

There are three basic components to medical care: quality, cost and access. Traditionally, physicians were trained to worry about only the first—providing the finest quality of care at whatever the cost. This was a sensible and practical approach for many reasons. Physicians could do best what they were trained to do and because costs, in real terms, not just taking into account inflation, were a tiny fraction of what they are today. Costs for diagnosis, treatment and hospital care could be covered in large part by health insurance at a relatively modest fee. Also the expense of doing business by a physician in his office was a tiny fraction of what it is today. When I was starting out in practice, my father's generation of physicians were still doing business out of offices in their homes, often doing their own billing (or collecting directly from the patient) and making do with one or two in help. Now physicians practice out of commercial buildings and pay the going business rates, require complete business offices with computerized systems to handle the maze of third party payments and pay astronomical and ever-rising fees for professional societies, mandated professional meetings, professional and business licenses, and of course liability insurance. Record keeping, both business and professional becomes ever more complex as our new paperless society requires more and more paper to document, justify, explain everything that is done. Liability insurance has become a nightmare all in its own right. When I was a resident, I was told that I had to have liability insurance, so for thirty-five dollars a year I had it. Now some specialists in some fields of specialization are paying close to $200,000 per year, and while the average is less, the dollar amounts for all are still staggering. As overhead approaches and even passes the 50 percent mark, with fees such as Medicare payments frozen, many if not most physicians are struggling to maintain their incomes, let alone see them rise.

As costs of health care have risen and therefore the costs of providing health insurance, third party payers have taken a more active role in providing health care. They decide on whether a second opinion is required for surgery; whether a patient should or should not be hospitalized and for how long; whether a test should or should not be performed; and whether care is or is not appropriate—if they determine that it is not, they will simply deny payment for the care. By making the insurance forms more complex, the language more abstruse, the justification more detailed, etc., the third party payers effectively delay payments for services to hospital, physician and patient. Whether or not the patient knows it, medical care is in effect being provided by people other than his or her own physician. These people may be nurses, claims adjusters, clerks or independent medical examiners, but they all have one thing in common: They do not know the patient. Physicians are certainly not above being questioned but it is demoralizing, to say the least, to have one's professional judgment second guessed at every turn by people who not only do not know the particular patient but are looking at them through a different lens—the lens of cost and not of quality.

Cost of health care is astronomical, but it must be seen as a universal problem of western societies. A rising tide of longer-lived patients with multiple medical problems, the deluge of sophisticated (and expensive) technologies and treatments, the rising numbers of health care professionals providing the care, the increased educational level of the population expecting (demanding would be closer to it) more and more care are common to these societies. Some try to control costs by ever-rising insurance premiums and larger co-insurance payments, others by rationing care, and virtually all by blaming the doctors for their improved state of health. It has to be understood that at bottom nobody wishes to pay for health care at all. It is the spending of one's assets from which one derives no pleasure. It would be far more gratifying to spend it on a new car, a vacation or virtually anything else. The more it takes away from pleasurable things, the more it is resented.

The third leg of the triad—access—was looked upon quite differently when I started medicine. While accepted that everyone should receive medical care, layering of such care was recognized as the norm. Those who could afford it were given special care with special amenities. Private rooms with private baths, specially prepared food, private duty nurses and other services were all available. Those without any means were cared for on the charity wards of the private teaching hospitals or at the city or county hospitals. A certain rough trade-off was made. Although the amenities were far less than described above and the physicians providing the primary care (interns and residents) were far less experienced than physicians in private practice, this was offset by the devotion and attention of these doctors-in-training as well as the nursing staffs who worked extremely hard under adverse conditions. In most of these institutions, there was a medical school affiliation and a system of hospital-based university physicians stationed at these institutions. These were supplemented by a clinical faculty made up of private practice physicians who spent time teaching to keep up their diagnostic skills, to come in contact with younger physicians and to maintain a university appointment and who provided the experience and back-up for physicians in training. Not a perfect system perhaps, but one that functioned reasonably well until overwhelmed by numbers of patients, costs of care, obsolescence of facilities, and changing societal mores about "fairness" and equality.

As usual, the middle class was caught in-between and did the best it could. These patients were able to pay enough to have private physicians and were hospitalized at private institutions, but they made do with four, six and eight beds per room, with a common bath. A day room was usually available with the lone television set on the floor. Phones, when available, were pay phones in the hall. Now it is accepted that everyone has the right to at least a semi-private motel-style room with private baths, TV and telephone, as well as access to every sophisticated method of diagnosis and treatment—hang the cost. That this has contributed to the staggering hospital per diem cannot be denied.

To see the current state of medicine and not recognize that physicians have been part of the problem would be totally unrealistic. With the advent of scientific medicine, physicians were trained to be scientists: aloof, dispassionate, concerned primarily with the disease process and not the patient. Objectivity is essential to the making of difficult decisions but clearly many carried it too far. This was interpreted, and indeed in many cases was, arrogance, haughtiness and lack of empathy for the patient. The pendulum is now swinging the other way and it is recognized that the art of medicine remains as important as the science of medicine, even in this technological age (perhaps even more importantly in this technological age), but the damage has been done.

Further, there is no question that greed has affected a part of the medical profession, as it has indeed all spheres of our society. The growth of third-party payments has reduced the restraints inherent in the financial contract between physician and patient, on both sides, but it is particularly reprehensible on the part of physicians—some physicians—to use third party payments to maximize income, and not patient care.

Things are never as simple as they seem on the surface. Many societal factors are at work which are beyond

167

the control of the individual physician. A mobile population breaks the bonds of longtime physician-patient relationships. Frequently a physician will live in one community, a patient in a second community and they will meet as physician/patient in a third community, a fact that tends to make the relationship more of a business transaction than a true relationship. The growth of specialization has in some cases reduced the role of primary care physician to that of gatekeeper. In many cases the patient as consumer selects his or her own specialist, and will then get a second opinion on the recommendation of the first specialist—often in a different community and without the primary care physician knowing about it—further breaking down the continuity of care. As physicians specialize and sub-specialize, they perforce focus on their area of expertise and see less and less of the total patient and his needs.

Public perception of physicians has clearly changed in my lifetime, and not for the better. Some of this is simple endemic to the practice of medicine, and always has been. Modern medicine has produced what I call the "Chevrolet Syndrome" where patients envision themselves as autos under warranty that they take to the medical mechanic to make perfect. Anything less than perfection—a perfect outcome from a surgery, a perfectly formed baby, a perfect recovery from an illness and obviously someone is at fault. That someone, of course, is the physician; and in our litigious society, there is of course only one way to solve the problem—the lawsuit with the hoped-for application of the green poultice.

The unreasonable demands and expectations placed on physicians by society would be humorous were they not so debilitating. Everyone yearns for the old days when physicians made house calls; at the same time, the physician is called on to be more efficient and there is hardly a less efficient way to provide quality health care than to make house calls. Patients deride overbooking of appointments but casually cancel these appointments at the last minute or simply fail to appear for an appointment. A physician has no product to sell, only his time and services. He is to keep on schedule but each patient expects the physician to spend the maximum time with him, explaining and re-explaining and justifying every diagnostic test and every treatment. More and more frequently the majority of time is spent resolving the patient's litigation problem, insurance problem, time away from work problem, job description problem, disability retirement problem and, only as an afterthought, the medical problem which brought him to the physician's office in the first place. Virtually all patients come to the office clutching pieces of paper which must be filled out or dictated immediately—if not sooner. The physician is told to run his office as a business and not a "cottage industry," but when he does behave like a businessman or entrepreneur he is accused of being money hungry and greedy. He is to be completely "au courant" with the mountainous scientific literature, deal with mountains of paperwork, keep perfect records, have an ideal family life, participate actively in the community and practice problem-free and perfect medicine—all at a lower cost of course.

Everybody is cost-conscious and rightly so. We should differ between the worried-well, those who want reassurance that nothing is wrong or that only something minor is wrong, as opposed to those with a serious disabling or life threatening disorder. In the latter category I have never in my entire career heard a patient ask me to refer him to the cheapest surgeon—only the best. I have never heard him/her ask to be admitted to the cheapest hospital—only the best. I have never been asked for the cheapest consultants—only the best. Cost control is important, of course, but only for the other guy.

The advent of modern technology has in many ways been a mixed blessing. It has clearly aided in diagnosis (particularly early diagnosis) as well as in treatment but often at the price of overuse and the sacrifice of a physician's own good sense and judgment. There is virtually no brake on ordering expensive diagnostic testing and treatment, and every incentive to order more and do more. In medical school and during residency training, one will seldom be criticized for ordering or doing something assuming one can come up with a reasonable rationale, but the preceptor will come down very hard on someone foolish enough not to order something—in the vernacular, to fail to do a thorough work-up. When a physician starts practicing medicine in the community, he or she wants to use the principles learned in school and in residency. He or she wants to practice "good scientific medicine." Everybody likes to employ and be conversant with the latest technology—nobody wants to be seen as an ignorant old-fashioned doctor. The patient participates in the pattern, asking for tests which were just touted in the lay press, often stating "Don't worry about it, Doc, my insurance will cover it." A physician can stand firm but if something appears that was not tested for, it will be virtually impossible to justify the withholding of the test or procedure on the witness stand. Defensive medicine to protect against lawsuits is a real and constant burden with which the physician deals on a daily basis and which guides all of his actions. As competition for patients becomes fiercer and fiercer, it becomes more and more difficult to deny the wishes of the patient and to risk losing him. When hospitals purchase new and expensive technology, pressure is put on physicians to utilize it to justify its presence.

Finally, a minority of physicians invest in technology that they employ in their practices. Physicians have always done that (EKG machines, X-ray machines, etc.) but now the technology is so expensive that it must be purchased and utilized by groups of physicians. The majority of those who have participated in the purchase of an expensive piece of equipment utilize the technology exactly the way they would if they were not investors (in virtually all cases the investments are small and the income represents only a tiny fraction of their total professional income), but there is no question that a few individuals utilize these investments as a license to steal; thus, the only force opposing the greater utilization of more and more expensive technologies is the personal satisfaction that one can draw from making a diagnosis with the least rather than the most usage of testing. One could say that this could be avoided by expanding the HMOs and Preferred Provider Organizations (PPOs) but here there exists a definite reverse economic incentive: The primary physicians divide up at the end of the year monies not spent, so there is a clear disincentive to order studies, refer to specialists, authorize treatments, all of which might well be necessary.

It is not often understood that after the capital commitment for the technology, the principal cost is salary for technicians. With a nationwide shortage of technicians, nurses and therapists, a dramatic rise in salaries has taken place. Perhaps these rises are justified, but these costs cannot be laid at the feet of the physicians. The physician is seen as the gatekeeper and therefore responsible for rising health care costs. This neglects, however, the rising tide of non-physician health care providers who practice independently of physicians, who order studies as do physicians and whose fees, adjusted for training and responsibility are comparable or more so than physician's fees.

The private practice of medicine has clearly become far more burdensome than it was when I started. Even the most cheerful, optimistic and dedicated amongst us cannot fail to see this. In the new paperless society, we are drowning in paperwork: longer and more detailed office and hospital notes (documentation is the current buzz word), letters to lawyers, to employers, to insurance carriers take up more and more time. The office staff, too, must produce more and more paperwork to justify everything the physician has done if he expects to get paid for his services. Overhead keeps rising and bumps up against freezes on fees. Lack of cohesion among physicians is caused by a number of factors. Overproduction of physicians (started by the government as a means of controlling costs but contributing wildly to escalating costs and the development of well-financed HMOs and PPOs) has brought about fierce competition among physicians. There has been an uneven distribution of the financial pie with some few specialties reaping gigantic rewards and most others struggling. As long as the pie grew this was not a major problem, but with it growing more slowly resentments have been fuelled. With increased specialization, sub-specialization and sub-sub-specialization, physicians tend less and less to speak a common language. Finally the government in the form of the Federal Trade Commission has said that physicians must compete or be sued for restraint of trade, something which does not lead to great camaraderie and sense of being part of the larger picture.

Overriding all is the specter of malpractice suits. It colors everything the physician does and how he feels about himself and his work. It is simply not true that if you just practice good medicine you will not be sued as it only affects a few "bad apples." The latter group may be sued with greater frequency but everyone, in all fields and providing all levels of care is subject to suit. It is, not of course, that physicians whatever their competence should be immune from taking responsibility for their deeds, nor that patients should not be compensated for errors, human though they may be. It is not even the cost, which is usually, although not always, covered by liability insurance—ever-increasing coverage at ever-increasing costs. It is the adversarial approach of a trial, preparations for which may take years, which so unnerves the physician. Most physicians understand that it is a money game. There are a few cases, of course, of obvious and gross malpractice but most cases result from less-than-optimum outcomes. Most of these are beyond the control of a physician; a few because everything that we are now capable of doing has a certain incidence of risk, something which the public subliminally recognizes but refuses to acknowledge when it happens personally. If you consider every action by a physician or other health care provider as a transaction, and this would include every test ordered or held off, every treatment started or stopped, every medicine given by a nurse in a hospital and many, many more, literally millions of transactions take place every day. Hundreds of millions if not billions of transactions take place every year. With a magnitude of this order, and dealing with very powerful but also very dangerous tools, the number of problems that do occur is remarkably small. Of course the media seizes on the more egregious of these faulty transactions and magnifies them so that they appear to be commonplace and everyday, whereas in reality they are not.

Although the physician realizes intellectually that this is the way things are played in America today (and it has extended far beyond physicians now), emotionally he is distraught because his very self-image as a healer is challenged. The endless hours of record reviews, attorney conferences and depositions culminating in a trial in which his entire image of self-worth is challenged is incredibly destructive. If he does not want to go through with that and agrees to a settlement, even if he knows that he has done nothing wrong, that also leads to feelings of guilt and cowardice. Very moving articles about what this process has done to physicians and their families during the ordeal have appeared recently. Before that physicians hid, not wishing to face their colleagues. The physicians are starting to come out of the closet now, to state their anguish and to start to set up self-help groups.

It is often asked why physicians do not do more to police themselves. There is no question but that, "There but for the grace of God go I," exists in the minds of all physicians. It is also true that bad or unfortunate outcomes are part of the practice of medicine and do not constitute malpractice per se. But physicians do make an attempt to weed out bad apples. This is done not only by the licensure boards but also by members of the hospital staffs, who spend enormous amounts of painful, difficult and uncompensated time to deal with these problems. The reward for this is often a lawsuit against these physicians, claiming that their sole motive is restraint of trade. Then additional hours over many years, at great additional cost, both emotional and financial, will be spent defending themselves.

174

It is with great sadness that I see the decline of my profession. Organized medicine and its practitioners could certainly have behaved better, but then again what group could not have? When people stand up and criticize, I ask myself, "What about your profession or occupation, is it truly better and nobler, freer from faults than mine?" There are very few who can answer in the affirmative. In a larger sense, do the faults not lie with society, as it relentlessly pursues the goal of ever more money obtained by whatever means possible and spent in as conspicuous a style as possible? Physicians live in the society and adopt the mores of the society. In fantasy, one would like to see physicians living a noble ascetic life of sacrifice, but we know that for what it is—fantasy. Those physicians who cross the line and break the law should be treated with the full penalty of the law. Those who adopt the values of a large part of society and permit greed to dominate all actions should be treated with contempt by their fellow professionals and by society. Society's expectations of outcomes are so unrealistic that they can never be met except by superhumans—superhumans who come cheap of course. It is very difficult to put your health and indeed your life in the hands of someone else, to reduce yourself again to the role of a child in the care of an adult, but never before has there been such questioning of the judgment of the physician at every turn. Being an intelligent consumer is important and even helpful as the patient participates in his care, but all too often it is carried to the extreme where a physician feels that it is impossible to exercise his best professional judgment, a very dangerous situation. Those who espouse the formation of a National Health Service turn livid when expounding on the fraud, waste and inefficiency at the

175

Pentagon. What do they think will happen when they set up a bureaucracy many times the size of the Pentagon?

We do not have to turn to non-medical models in this country to try and see how a National Health System might work. We have several federal agencies providing health care as well as state and municipal agencies. All of these strive mightily within their limitations to provide the best care possible. There are many dedicated professionals within these organizations but here, as everywhere, it is the flow of feet that counts. Are people in the private sector rushing to have their care delivered by these agencies or is it the opposite: people making every effort to have their care delivered in the private sector?

How will society benefit if physicians feel themselves besieged on all sides? A beleaguered profession is not one that will long attract a nation's best and brightest, as already seen by a declining number of applicants to medical school. It is inherently one of nature's noble endeavors and will therefore always attract dedicated men and women. The best will look forward to university posts or research positions, while those who do engage in primary care will more and more become employees of one system or another. There is nothing fundamentally wrong with being an employee, but inevitably more and more time and concern will revolve around benefits, for the employee and not for the patient. With salaries fixed, energies will be diverted to the establishment of a new pecking order based on who has the longest waiting list of patients, who controls the largest number of hospital beds, who has the largest house staff, who controls the most research funds and so on. I personally have seen this behavior happen.

For those treating outpatients, if a choice has to be made between attending an interesting conference or treating patients at a busy clinic, where do you think the physician will end up? If the choice is between spending a lot of time with an interesting problem or treating a large number of routine and mundane problems, where do you think the salaried physician's time and energy will be directed? If there are complaints now about waiting time in physician's offices, lack of personalized attention, returning of phone calls and attention to the patient's paperwork, how much worse will it be when the physician is salaried? I except from this those salaried physicians who staff our world famous large medical clinics and where the highest quality patient care is deemed essential to the mission of the clinic. And where it is indeed provided.

An easy solution to the many problems pertaining to medical care is certainly not in sight, but the changes, it seems to me, have to come more from changes in societal values and perceptions than it does from continuously enacting new legislation. A more realistic expectation of the limitations of what medicine and physicians themselves can do, of the inevitability of less-than-perfect outcomes, and indeed, the likelihood of some level of complications and even outright errors has to be expected. Compensation for patients who have been wronged must be arranged, but the tort system is clearly not the way to do it. Finally, society's approach to physicians must undergo a change, not for the sake of the physicians but for the sake of society. It may gratify some to continually paint physicians as greedy, uncaring and unfeeling monsters but that will surely be a self-fulfilling prophesy. Shouldn't we use the stick to strongly punish the minority of transgressors but the carrot to encourage physicians to do the best they can for their patients?

Physicians I Have Known

Throughout my medical career, I have known many physicians. Some I have known well and then there have been many, many more I have just known casually or even just observed. My observations of these people is not based on whether I liked them or not, and not even on whether they were medically competent (most were). Incidentally, one does not get into medical school, and certainly does not complete medical school without being bright. However, there seems to be little correlation between the level of brightness and how well one functions as a physician. As students we were in agreement that some of our brightest classmates were not fit to treat anybody or anything. Fortunately, there is always research. My comments here go more to character than to levels of medical achievement.

By and large, I was tremendously impressed with physicians as a group. They were honest, truly interested in their work, anxious to improve their level of knowledge and incredibly industrious. They were certainly devoted to their patients and their welfare, and genuinely pleased when they were able to help someone, but what impressed me the most of all was their willingness to sacrifice. One could not go to the hospital at any time of the day or night, weekends, holidays, summer or winter without finding physicians there. They were busy making rounds, seeing emergencies, working in the operating room or just completing charts in the record room. Surely they would rather be elsewhere. Surely they realized that they were sacrificing what has come to be known as "quality time" with their families. All of this of course was in addition to the regular workday that was long and hard enough as it is. Yet they did what had to be done with little complaint, understanding that that was the nature of their profession.

Yet I also observed some very unpleasant qualities in some few of the physicians I knew. I am not talking about the outright scoundrels. I knew of a few of those who had served time in the pokey for such things as income tax fraud, Medicare fraud and false testing of clinical research studies. I read in the bulletins of the state boards of medicine disciplinary panels about even worse things. I am not even talking about the few—the very few—who were truly careless and sloppy in their work and appeared to regard what they were doing as merely a job rather than a calling. No, I am talking about some physicians who exhibited such poor character traits that I could not help but wonder how and why they had entered medicine at all. Surely other fields would have been better suited for their talents. They were petty, jealous, mean spirited, and constantly conniving and scheming. They spent precious energy on planning how to do in their fellow physicians, rather than concentrating on the job at hand, namely the providing of quality care to their patients. They were usually very political and would do anything to advance up the political ladder, no matter how unimportant such things appeared to me to be.

I found myself always wondering why. There was more than enough work for everyone. I found that the practice of medicine itself took up all my energy. Why waste one's time on nonsense. I guess the answer was what I thought it to be—bad character.

Salute

Anyone who has been in the military knows that it is the master sergeants and the chief petty officers who make the military function. On a day-to-day basis, the fundamentals of recruitment, training, supply, unit cohesion and often small unit tactics falls upon the senior NCOs. For long periods of time officers may be all but invisible, with the senior NCOs running the show. Good NCOs provide good morale, while poor NCOs do the opposite. That being the case, why do they, the NCOs, salute the officers—that is, accept the officer's superior status?

The answer is that beyond the efficient functioning of the small unit which falls under the purview of the NCO, the larger functions of the military fall to the officer corps. These include larger unit tactics, strategy, co-ordination of larger systems, overall preparedness, major equipment and weapons systems purchases, testimony before civilian overseers and many other functions. This is a result of superior education, of both a military and non-military nature, as well as promotion with rising rank to ever-larger responsibilities. That is why they are in charge, why they are saluted and why they earn their pay.

In many ways there are similarities with the provision of health care. In earlier days, physicians functioned essentially alone. Nowadays, no physician can function alone—he or she is dependent upon the services of non-physicians for the appropriate care of the patient. This is true in the office, but even more so in the hospital. The day-to-day care, as well as observations regarding the progress or lack thereof of the patient is the function of the nursing staff. I say staff, for here too responsibility is layered, with Registered Nurses (RNs) assuming charge over Licensed Practical Nurses (LPNs), nursing aides, clerical staff, volunteers and a raft of other people who come in contact with the patient such as cleaning staff, maintenance staff, orderlies and a wide assortment of technicians. These technicians provide the backbone for the diagnostic procedures which must be performed while a range of therapists provide the necessary treatment without which the patient will not reach maximum recovery. This says nothing about the dieticians who determine what the patient will eat as well as the pharmacists and pharmacy assistants who provide the necessary medicines and many, many more.

So what is the role of the physician in this entire complex program which makes up hospital care? He or she establishes the diagnosis out of a sometimes confusing differential diagnosis. He or she orders the sophisticated tests which are often necessary to establish the diagnosis, and does so in the appropriate order. He or she directs the treatment, which is often complex and dangerous. Multiple diseases present in the individual provide even more complex problems to deal with. Which treatments to use, and whether or not they should be used is his responsibility. Obviously, when surgery is required it is performed by a physician, albeit not without a complex support system. When things go wrong it becomes the responsibility of the physician, even if said physician did not physically do anything wrong. Have you ever heard of any health personnel being sued without the concomitant suit of the attending (and any other physician involved in the care of the patient) physician? It simply doesn't happen. Finally the cessation of treatment when that is appropriate and the dealing with the family is the responsibility of the physician.

With the growth and multiplication of caregivers, each profession wishes to take more and more responsibility for the providing of care, many wishing to provide such care completely independently from physicians. There are few specialties of medicine which do not have non-physician caregivers competing with them, claiming that they can provide the same care, but cheaper. Oftentimes they are right. Many problems are simple, some are self-limited, some respond better to the often-superior personal attention provided by non-physician caregivers. The problem arises when apparently simple, straightforward problems are the harbingers of a more serious problem which is not recognized by non-physicians who do not have the more global view of health care problems which physicians, as a result of their education and training, do have.

It is important for physicians to tuck in their egos and admit that they do not know everything. Indeed they cannot know everything, given the explosion of medical and health knowledge. They therefore have to learn how to say "I don't know," and refer the patient out, even to non-physicians, who should get a respectful hearing when they venture an opinion. Further, physicians cannot do everything. They therefore must rely on others who do certain things better. Finally, the issue of cost. Needless to say, medicine is extremely expensive. But then again, life and health are extremely valuable. The more complex the problem, the more one needs the services of the one who is saluted—the physician.

Specialty Wars

I suppose it is just human nature, but I would look on with a mixture of awe and dismay at the constant battles being fought within medicine. I, for one, found it difficult enough just keeping up with my medical practice, but there were clearly those who not only fought but also actually relished such battles. Although all of the various specialties were involved, it was most often the surgeons who were engaged in such endeavors. There is indeed clearly such a thing as a surgical personality.

This first came to my attention when I took a job at a municipal hospital, my first job after my residency and my military service. As a department head, I was invited to attend staff meetings. These were eye openers. Remember, everyone there was on salary, so it was not money they were fighting over, which would have been understandable. Rather, it was turf. Who would control more wards and more beds? Who would have more residency positions? Who would have more staffing slots to fill? And so on. There were battles with the Health Department, which had authority over the hospital, and liked to exercise it. There were battles with outside attending physicians from the local universities who had set up separate fiefdoms at the city hospital complex and wished to keep them. There were battles between different hospitals in the municipal hospital system and there were battles within the main hospital complex, particularly between the general hospital and the psychiatric hospital.

When I left government employment to begin work in the private sector, the battles continued, although they were somewhat different. They weren't so much about turf as they were about power and of course income. Bitter battles were fought between specialties as to who would be allowed to do various procedures, meaning of course about who would get the income. Having power meant, among other things, deciding who would have the desirable operating times, who would get preferential admission for their patients when bed space was tight and who would set policies for the hospital.

When our group went to the administration with a proposal to set up an imaging procedure, we were fought tooth and nail by the radiology group who claimed that they were in charge of imaging procedures. Did they know anything about this procedure? No. Did they intend doing the procedure? No. Did they even believe in the efficacy and usefulness of the procedure? No. But they were in charge of imaging and they and nobody else would do imaging procedures. Doctors were not above dirty tricks either. I recall that long before anyone else even thought of it, I proposed setting up a sports medicine facility at the hospital. At first this was greeted enthusiastically, but within a short period of time there were those who were busy maneuvering behind my back to take charge of the clinic.

One would think that with all this fighting there would be no energy left for other fighting but one would be wrong. By far the most bitter fighting took place between physicians and those non-physicians who were seen as encroaching on their turf. This was certainly not completely unjustified since people with lesser training wished to do the same things as physicians, and most physicians felt that these people were not really qualified to do these things. In most cases the physicians honestly felt that they were preserving standards and protecting the public, and I believe they were in the main correct. All had stories about foul ups by non-physicians who had gotten in over their head and required the physician to solve the problem as best he could. However, it cannot be denied that there were bread and butter issues at stake as well, which made the fighting particularly vicious. If physicians ceded the simpler procedures to non-physicians and took on only the most complex problems, there would simply not be enough income to have a successful practice since most of medical practice was made up of the simple bread and butter problems. One could not charge enough of a fee on the complex issue to make up for the loss of the majority of the practice. The ophthalmologists did everything possible to fight off the optometrists, while the orthopedists did the same with the podiatrists and the chiropractors. The physiatrists fought with the physical therapists while the obstetricians feuded with the nurse midwifes. The anesthesiologists feuded with the nurse anesthetists, the general practitioners with the nurse practitioners, the otolaryngologists with the audiologists and the psychiatrists with the clinical psychologists. To be honest, it was also a question of authority and status as well as income.

I don't know where they got the energy and the time but I guess there is nothing like a good battle to bring out the best or worst in people.

Epilogue

It has been a long career and an even longer acquaintance with medicine, inasmuch as my father was a physician and kept his office practice on the first floor of our house. In this book, I have mixed my own personal perceptions of what medicine and medical practice was really about with musings about the larger issues of health care. I do not for a minute deny that other people in other disciplines have opinions—worthy opinions—about health care and how to deal with the myriad problems surrounding the delivery of health care. However, reading, writing, research and careful thought are not a substitute for being in the trenches and experiencing these problems on a daily basis. It was not comprehensible to me that the government, under the guidance of Hillary Clinton, undertook the reform of our entire health care system without turning to those who deal with these problems every day of our lives, and for whom changes had real-life consequences. I am not just talking about pocketbook issues but the actual delivery of care. The only sensible explanation for that omission is that those who were doing the planning had preconceived notions as to how the results should come out and practicing physicians might point out certain realities which would prevent the implementation of those preconceived ideas.

Now that I am retired, I frequently ask myself the question "Would I do it again? Would I choose medicine

186

as a career?" After all, enormous sacrifices were made to become a physician and to actually practice as a physician. My retired colleagues all ask themselves the same question, and for the most part their answer is yes, although with some doubts and some qualifications to their answers. To even ask the question is strange since in past times the answer would be an unqualified yes, without any doubt and any hesitation.

The reason we would all unhesitatingly have said yes to a career in medicine if the question were posed in the fifties, sixties and seventies is that medicine answered our needs. We were interested in providing a service, and medicine was as good a service as one could provide. It was intellectually challenging. For those who wished to do so, they could practice on their own and be the masters of their own fate, working when and how hard they chose, running their office the way that they saw fit. A comfortable living could be earned (in spite of stories to the contrary, most physicians earned comfortable, but not exorbitant incomes). Finally, we were treated with respect by most people who recognized that we had made enormous sacrifices to acquire the knowledge and skills necessary to help them. Further, there was respect for our motives that were not seen simply as a means to enrich ourselves.

The last few decades have brought all of the assumptions we held in doubt. Our motives became suspect. Our patients were seen as potential enemies, rather than people who needed our help. The ever-present threat of lawsuits colored what we did, what we said, what we wrote. Our energies were diverted by the need to justify our actions to insurance companies who would deny what we felt to be appropriate care for that particular patient. Not a very happy environment in which to work. And why would anyone choose to work in such an environment?

All of which leads one to wonder what is good for the country's health care in the future. It is axiomatic that everyone will be ill at some time in his or her life. To provide for that inevitability, they should want in place a first-rate health system at all levels—and that certainly includes first rate physicians. The falling number of applications to medical school with the ultimate result of falling quality of applicants and thus acceptances does not bode well for health care in the future. The falling number of registered nurses available already places quality hospital care at risk. Do we really want the same thing for physicians? And what are we to make of the changing attitudes amongst physicians? Professionalism is out and trade unionism is in. Salaried employment, regular hours, other benefits, avoidance risks, and counting down the time to retirement all pervade medicine at this time. That just can't be good for quality medical care.

It is necessary to focus on the basics of what is really important to us as a society and how to go about getting it. Good health care goes along with a good education and the provision of adequate public safety as the keys to a happy and successful society. We should make every effort to see that we have these in hand before working and worrying about other things.